A SKYLARK IN BLUE YONDER

Jon Brownridge

Published by

MELROSE BOOKS

An Imprint of Melrose Press Limited
St Thomas Place, Ely
Cambridgeshire
CB7 4GG, UK
www.melrosebooks.com

FIRST EDITION

Copyright © Jon Brownridge 2007

The Author asserts his moral right to
be identified as the author of this work

Cover designed by Jeremy Kay

ISBN 978 1 906050 30 6

Printed and bound in Great Britain by:
Cromwell Press, Aintree Avenue, White Horse Business Park,
Trowbridge, Wiltshire, BA14 0XB, UK

Remembering Peter and Tom

A SKYLARK IN BLUE YONDER

Contents

I
TOUCHING THE ENGLISH SKY

'Any passengers who want to 'elp, come on over 'ere!' bellowed the burly, red-faced Yorkshireman, jumping from his truck and grinning from ear to ear. 'We need all the 'elp we can get.'

Stomping briskly through the wet grass, he opened the tailgate of the well-used trailer and started to pull out a large, green canvas bag. His companion quickly joined him and between the two of them they managed to pull the heavy bag to the ground.

I looked around at the crowd of twenty or so people on either side of me. They were all watching the proceedings with excited anticipation, but no one seemed to be moving. I thought perhaps I was the only passenger present, so with some trepidation I walked forward, trying to look casual and relaxed.

'Hi,' I said to the Yorkshireman, 'I'm Jon. I talked to you on the phone this morning.'

'So you did!' he responded with great enthusiasm, which I had not expected. He dropped his side of the bag and quickly removed the dirty glove from his right hand. 'Brian Turner. I'm your pilot for the flight this evening.' He grabbed my hand and shook it vigorously, smiling all the while and treating me like a long-lost friend. 'Have you been in a hot-air balloon before?'

'Never,' I said. 'In fact I don't know anything about balloons, but I do have my ultralight aeroplane licence.'

1

'Ultralights!' he thundered. 'You can keep them bloody things. Too noisy and dangerous if you ask me.' He looked at his fellow balloonist, nodding his head with a grin as if looking for agreement. 'Eh, Dave?'

Dave was obviously a quieter type but he agreed with Brian Turner's assessment with a nod and a short chuckle.

'Dave's my chaser tonight,' boomed the balloon pilot, shaking the man's shoulder and then slapping him heartily on the back. 'We'll be safe as 'ouses with 'im.'

'Chaser?' I enquired. "What do they do?'

'They chase! What the 'ell do you think?'

I left it at that, not wanting to appear too green.

As Brian and his chaser resumed their work I was aware of the crowd of spectators following our conversation some twenty feet behind us. They were here to watch the balloon launch for its flight across the Yorkshire Dales, and they obviously knew that it took off from this same spot on the edge of Grassington at the same time every evening, weather permitting. I looked around and smiled weakly.

'What time are you taking off?' asked a young fellow with a baseball cap perched backwards on his head. He seemed to think I knew exactly what I was doing.

'In about an hour,' I told him confidently, enjoying my new status as someone who knew about balloons.

Brian and Dave pulled out a large wicker basket and started to drag it across the grass. 'Come on, then, if you want to 'elp.' Brian's round face looked redder than ever. 'We should be off the ground in 'alf an hour.'

Things moved very quickly after that. I helped drag out the colourful balloon from its bag and we spread it along the ground like an enormous snake. I was astonished at its length and at the amount of material that had been used to construct it. By now, two other passengers had arrived, a young couple in their twenties, and they too were soon involved in preparing the balloon for flight.

'Right, luv! Can you start pulling the fabric from underneath?' Brian led the young woman to the other side of the balloon and showed her how to grab the material from underneath and spread it flatly on the ground. 'What's your name, luv?'

'Linda,' she told him. 'My name's Linda. And my husband's name is Bob.'

'Right, then! Keep pulling from underneath. Bob, you can do the same from your side.'

Brian headed back to where I was standing, pulling out large sections of balloon fabric here and there along the way. When he reached me he pointed to the mouth of the balloon where Dave was unravelling the long steel cables attached to the envelope.

'You can 'elp Dave, if you like,' he said. 'Hold the mouth open so he can pump some cold air in.'

Dave connected the ends of the cables to the upright posts protruding from the corners of the basket, using solid steel karabiners to secure them. As I pulled open the mouth of the balloon he moved over to a large motorized fan that was set to one side. The fan's propeller was about three feet across and it was safely encaged behind a sturdy-looking wire-mesh frame.

'What do we do with this, then?' I asked cautiously. 'Is this what pushes the balloon along?'

'Hell, no!' said Dave, highly amused at my naïve question. 'This is the cold inflation fan. We'll get the balloon about three quarters full with this before we light the burners for the hot inflation. Hold that mouth open and we'll get started.'

A couple of sharp pulls on the starter cord and the fan came noisily to life. Dave adjusted the fan's position slightly to direct the powerful blast towards the centre of the opening I had created. What had started as a long snake on the ground now began to grow and expand at an alarming rate as the fan did its job. The balloon quickly transformed into an enormous marquee, and it was all I could do to hold the edge of the mouth in position, grabbing the steel cables for extra leverage. A swell of excitement swept over me. The sheer size and power of this gentle giant was truly amazing.

'My God!' I yelled over the deafening roar of the fan. 'You could hold a wedding reception in here.' Dave smiled but did not respond. Leaving the fan, he walked over to Bob and brought him to the other side of the mouth showing him how to hold it high, allowing the rush of air to enter.

'Excuse me! I'm Jason. Are you the pilot?' I jumped at the shock of someone shouting in my ear. I looked around at the newcomer and laughed.

'No!' I yelled back. 'I'm one of the passengers.'

He grinned, slightly embarrassed. 'So am I,' he mouthed over the din. 'Passenger, that is. What are we supposed to do?'

'You'll have to talk to Brian Turner. He's the pilot.'

Jason went to find our pilot who was now hidden by the half-inflated balloon. Despite the roar of the fan, however, I soon heard the same enthusiastic welcome that I had received twenty minutes earlier. I grinned over at Bob with raised eyebrows and shrugged shoulders when I heard this, thinking this must be the standard greeting for everyone.

As we held the balloon mouth wide open we were not able to converse over the fan's roar, but through body language and facial expression we marvelled at this amazing craft that would soon take us to the sky.

Suddenly, Brian Turner appeared back at the mouth.

'Almost ready now,' he beamed, his round, grinning face filled with enthusiasm and excitement.

I watched him climb into the tipped basket, settling himself into a position he was obviously well used to. He fiddled with the valve taps on the large propane tanks that supplied the fuel and then, grabbing the double burners with his gloved hands, he pulled them into position and pointed them at the centre of the opening that Bob and I had created. After a few hefty adjustments, pulling the burners back and forth to find the optimum position, he lit the pilot lights on each one with two or three presses of the red piezo buttons. He seemed well satisfied with this and gave us a vigorous nod and a thumbs-up signal, indicating that he was ready to start.

'Hot inflation coming up! Hold that mouth wide open!'

I was totally unprepared for what happened next. As the powerful double burners blasted heat into the balloon I thought I must surely be in the wake of a jet plane. The shock of it caused me to jump back instantly, and much to the delight of the crowd of spectators, I stumbled and sat down heavily on the ground. Brian Turner had obviously enjoyed this reaction many times before and he could barely contain himself. He motioned with his hand to bring me back to the mouth.

'Never fails, that one! Pretty loud, eh?'

With my heart pumping like a steam hammer and an embarrassed smile on my face, I returned to my position. Bob looked equally shocked but somehow he had managed to hold on. Between the two of us we were able hold the mouth wide open, allowing Brian to complete the hot inflation without further incident.

As more heat was pumped into the balloon the enormous power of hot air began to take over. For the first time I saw a more serious expression developing on the pilot's face. This was serious business now and a measure of skill and concentration was needed. Slowly, the balloon began to rise to its upright position and the basket was pulled from its side so that the base now sat firmly on the ground.

'Turn that fan off!' Brian yelled above the roar. 'The red switch! Turn it off!'

I stepped over to the fan and grabbed the sturdy frame. By sheer coincidence I put my finger on the right switch and turned it off. Suddenly, everything seemed remarkably quiet, and in the relative silence a flurry of last-minute, almost panicky activity got under way.

Dave had been holding the balloon down with a long rope extending from the crown. Now he rushed over to the basket and attached the end of this crown line to one of the karabiners. He placed his body weight on the side of the basket to hold it down, at the same time keeping his feet firmly on the ground.

A yellow, fireproof scoop extended from the mouth of the balloon which was now well above the pilot's head. Dave quickly pulled it down and clipped it into place while Brian continued to pump hot air into the enormous envelope with intermittent blasts from the powerful burners. Suddenly, everything seemed ready to go.

'Passengers!' yelled Brian. 'Passengers, climb into the basket, one at a time!'

The four of us rushed to the basket with excited anticipation. A step built into the side allowed us to climb in with relative ease and with a helping hand from Dave we were soon installed in our positions, one on each of the four sides. Brian was leaning into one corner where he seemed to have an impressive array of instruments, a radio with microphone, and easy access to a red line extending to the top of the balloon.

'Welcome aboard!' he said after an extra long blast of the burners. 'You each have a rope handle in front of you. Hang on to it if you need to steady yourself.' He blasted again, using only one burner this time. 'We're almost ready now.'

Several short blasts followed, each lasting only two or three seconds. I felt a definite buoyancy developing, as if the basket were trying to break away. Dave partially removed his weight and the basket lifted two or three inches from the ground.

'You have lift,' he told the pilot and immediately leaned heavily on the basket again.

Brian again feathered the burners, giving several short blasts with only a second or two between. 'OK, Dave, let us go. We're off! Up into blue yonder!'

As Dave removed his weight from the basket the balloon slowly and silently rose from the ground. I was speechless as I gazed in wonder at the retreating ground below. The crowd of spectators broke into spontaneous applause, waving and cheering as the five of us headed for the clear blue sky.

Soon the crowd was but an assembly of tiny insects on the edge of a miniature town, and as the magnificent craft rose higher in the sky I could see dinky cars inching their way along winding ribbons of highway. In the distant fields and meadows tiny cows were grazing, and as we slowly gained altitude the glorious and unique vistas of the Yorkshire Dales came into view.

Neither pilot nor passengers had spoken a word since take-off, but now, after the tense activity of the final few minutes on the ground, a peace and tranquillity fell over the balloon and I finally found my voice.

'Wow!' I exclaimed, still quite awestruck and needlessly clinging to my rope handle. 'This is the most incredible thing I've ever done in my whole life!'

Linda and Bob were now together on one side of the basket, excitedly trying to identify a small lake that lay ahead, directly in our flight path. Brian blasted the burners, then joined in their conversation.

'That's Malham Tarn you're looking at,' he said, shading his eyes with one hand while keeping the other firmly on the burners. 'You can see Settle five or six miles away to the left, and beyond that is Lancashire. It looks like we're heading north-west tonight towards Pen-y-Ghent; that's the prominent flat-topped hill you can see way in the distance. My guess is we'll be landing in Moughton Fell with this wind speed.'

This puzzled me somewhat, and Jason looked a little taken aback too.

'You mean we're not going back to Grassington? I thought we'd be landing there.'

After a momentary stunned silence Brian roared with laughter and slapped me on the back several times. 'You don't mean to tell me you thought we could turn this balloon around?' he exclaimed with shameless hilarity. 'And you an ultralight pilot too!'

Jason noticed my embarrassment and he looked relieved that he hadn't asked the same question himself.

'No,' Brian went on. 'Balloons fly with the wind. We go whichever way the wind blows, and the distance we travel depends entirely on the wind speed.'

'So you can't steer a balloon at all, then?' asked Jason. 'How do you land?'

'We do have some control. We have precision control over altitude and, as a general rule, a higher altitude takes us to the right and a lower altitude to the left. When it comes to landing we look for fields on the left, two or three miles ahead.' He blasted the burners for several seconds. 'I'm talking too much,' he said. 'We're falling too fast.'

For an hour and a quarter we flew in this awesome craft. I savoured every minute of it, totally enthralled by the experience of flying so gently and calmly with only the occasional burner blast and our animated conversations to break the silence.

Brian, despite his boisterous nature and over-the-top personality, was the perfect pilot and guide. He took us as high as a mile and as low as six feet from the ground. We observed herds of deer, lone foxes on their evening hunt and a variety of birds flying below us. Brian pointed out dales and fells, lakes and rivers, and towards the end of the flight he identified for us the villages of Helwith Bridge, Studfold and Horton. Then, true to his word, he showed us our landing spot ahead – on the edge of Moughton Fell!

'There's where we land,' our pilot announced triumphantly, pointing to a large grassy field ahead. 'And what do you know? Here comes the chaser.'

We were now a mere 500 feet from the ground. Looking down on the road below, I could see the white truck slowly making its way to our landing spot. I leaned over to Jason and out of Brian's earshot I whispered, 'So that's what chasers do. They follow the balloon on its one-way trip and pick us up when we land. Dave will be driving us back to Grassington.'

Jason nodded with an enlightened expression. 'Now I get it,' he said quietly.

Our pilot grasped the red deflation line in his left hand and positioned himself at the front of the basket, his right hand grasping the burner control handle.

'OK, this is the time to hang on to those handles,' he said nonchalantly.

Brian concentrated on his target as the balloon slowly approached the meadow below. I could see the intensity in his face as he carefully feathered the burners, precisely controlling the rate of fall so that this incredible flying machine would touch down in the exact spot he had chosen. I marvelled at his skill and expertise as the balloon bounced softly along the ground before gently settling into the short grass.

'Stand-up landing,' Brian announced. 'Too bad we couldn't 'ave 'ad a good drag landing; you'd 'ave loved that, but there's not enough wind.'

I wasn't sure what he meant by a drag landing, but I was too filled with the excitement of the flight to ask for an explanation.

At that moment, Dave drove through the nearby gateway that luckily contained no gate and made his way towards us in the chase vehicle. He stopped a few feet short and jumped down, slamming the truck door with a loud bang. 'How was the flight?' he asked cheerily.

That was all we needed. The four of us, still standing in the basket, talked as one. We competed with one another to describe the awe and wonder we'd experienced flying in a balloon. We told of the sights we had seen, the wildlife, the birds, and the incredible magic of the Dales. Dave listened, smiling and nodding, but something told me he'd heard it all before.

'Right, then, let's get this thing down.' Brian handed the crown line to Dave, then he closed down the valves on the propane tanks. The pilot lights on the burners shut down with a gentle pop.

'You four can start getting out now – one at a time. Linda, you're first.'

Linda climbed out of the basket followed by her husband. The balloon was cooling rapidly and Brian seemed anxious to get us all out before it started to collapse on him.

'Come on, then,' he said. 'Jason, you can 'op out now. Stay with the basket, though, in case we need your weight. Jon, you stay with me and 'elp to tip the basket.'

Jason awkwardly climbed over the side of the basket, grappling with the flying wires as he did so. Once on the ground he leaned heavily on the side of the basket as directed.

Dave was now ready for action. Heaving with all his might on the crown line, he began to pull the huge envelope to the ground. At the same time Brian pulled out the parachute top with the red deflation line. The basket slowly tipped onto its side as the balloon fell. I grabbed a rope handle to steady myself. The burners had cooled down now and Brian and I were able to crawl out onto the grass. The flight was over, but I knew instinctively that this was the first of many. An ambitious idea was already forming in my mind.

Straddling the balloon at the mouth, Brian worked his way along its entire length until every last bit of air had been squeezed out. Everyone pitched in to fold the material back into its bag, which we then lifted onto the back of the truck. The basket and burners followed and within a few more minutes everything was loaded and ready to go.

'That's that, then,' said Brian, closing the tailgate with a noisy clatter. 'One more thing to do, though. Dave, where's the champagne?'

Reaching into the cab, Dave produced two bottles of champagne and a box containing several glasses. He handed the bottles to Brian and gave each of us a glass. 'This is a compulsory celebration after every balloon flight,' he joked. 'It's a two-hundred-year-old tradition.'

With a loud pop, the first bottle was uncorked, and as the champagne foamed and fizzed, Brian messily filled each of our glasses and then his own. 'To all balloonists everywhere,' he said reverently, holding up his glass. 'To the landowners who so graciously receive us. And to those who have flown in a balloon for the very first time.'

We shared in this toast with great enthusiasm and delight. All of us felt genuine friendship and bonding with our fellow passengers as we sipped champagne in that field on the edge of Moughton Fell. Our excited chatter continued and the time passed quickly. It was getting late now and it was time to go.

Jason and I both had wives waiting for us in Grassington and we wondered what they must be thinking about our long absence. I had told Naomi that the flight would be about an hour or so, but like me, she assumed we'd be landing in Grassington about an hour after take-off. We had already been gone more than two hours and we still had a lengthy drive back along the narrow, winding country roads.

Dave quickly packed the last few items and soon we were on our way. At this point Brian finally relaxed, settling himself into a corner of the back seat and leaving the challenging drive along the country lanes to Dave who seemed to be well used to it. We were all exhausted now, quieter than before, and feeling immensely satisfied with our amazing experience.

Soon, Linda and Bob were dozing between Brian and me, and Jason seemed to be nodding off in the front passenger seat. But my brain was working overtime as a curious plan continued to develop in my mind.

Brian looked over at me as the truck bounced and swayed along the country road, gently throwing me from side to side. 'So what's this American accent thing?' he said. 'Where are you from?'

I laughed. 'Not American,' I said. 'It's a bit of Canadian you're hearing. Believe it or not, I was born in Leeds. I'm a Yorkshireman, but I've been living in Canada for the last twenty years. I'm over here on holiday for three weeks.'

Brian sat up, adjusting his bulky frame on the narrow back seat. 'Canada, eh? What do you do out there? Build igloos?' He laughed at his own weak joke.

'I'm a teacher,' I said. 'A school principal, actually – you know, headmaster.'

'Well, rather you than me,' Brian said, shamelessly indulging in an enormous yawn.

'As a matter of fact,' I added, 'I've just been appointed to one of the roughest schools in town. I'll be starting there in September.'

'That sounds like fun. What part of Canada are you in?'

'Southern Ontario. My wife and I both teach in Toronto, but we live in a small town about fifteen miles outside. It's been a great twenty years. We love Canadians, and we've got used to the North American way of life.'

The conversation soon petered out. We were both tired and Brian obviously knew very little about Canada. I didn't want to bore him with any further details.

As we pulled into Grassington the main street was full of life and activity as holidaymakers strolled in the pleasant summer evening. As we approached the far side of town I could see Naomi talking to another woman and gazing out across the village green where we had lifted off some three hours earlier. Jason was wide-awake now. He wound down his window and peered out. 'There's Jean,' he said with some consternation. 'She'll wonder what the hell happened.'

Dave gently pulled into a laneway opposite the launch site, and the two women rushed over immediately, recognizing the balloon truck and trailer. They were obviously annoyed and relieved at the same time. Naomi grabbed my hand as I stepped from the truck.

'Where have you been?' she said. 'I've been waiting here for nearly two hours!'

'Blue yonder!' I said. 'We've been to blue yonder, and I can't wait to tell you about it. Sorry I'm so late back. I know now that balloon flights are one-way trips. We had to be picked up by the chaser and driven back. And then there was the champagne. . .. I have so much to tell.'

After hurried goodbyes and heart-felt thanks to the crew, Naomi and I were back on our way to Leeds. I told her about the incredible experience of flying in a balloon; the wildlife and birds we had seen from the air; the hauntingly magnificent and incomparable Yorkshire Dales; the fells and woodland that we had crossed. I excitedly described the thrill of seeing Pen-y-Ghent from above and the unique experience of crossing a lake a mere two feet above the water. She listened in wonder, wishing perhaps that she had joined me after all.

'And there's one more thing I have to tell you,' I said finally.

'And what would that be?' she asked with a familiar, suspicious tone in her voice.

'I'm going to be a hot-air balloon pilot!'

II
BALLOONS, PILOTS AND INSTRUCTORS

The weather was hot, humid and sticky in southern Ontario that year, but by the time we returned to Canada the summer was almost over and the first day of school was looming. I had already met the staff at my new school, and as I had made a point of completing all essential paperwork before going to England, everything seemed to be under control. I felt well prepared to take over Stanley Dunn Public School despite its reputation as a difficult place in a run-down neighbourhood. Class lists, enrolment figures, consumable supplies and textbook requirements were all in order, and teacher assignments had all been finalized.

I had four new teachers on staff, replacements for others who had requested transfers, and although I had met a handful of parents, the pleasure of meeting the parent committee was yet to come. This was my second school as principal and I was very familiar with the routines. I was greatly looking forward to the challenge, but I was sure I would have my hands full. It was because of the anticipated stress and pressure of the job that I would need a new interest, and I had firmly decided that hot-air ballooning was the answer for me. All I needed now was a training companion and I knew just the right man.

It was the week before school when I finally phoned Peter Broderick. I knew he'd be busy preparing for the new school year, but I couldn't wait any longer to tell him about my balloon flight in England and my plans to do some pilot training in Canada. He was always up for a new challenge. We both lived in Duffins Creek, and I guessed he would jump at the opportunity to join me.

'Can you meet me at the Black Dog?' I asked him. 'I've got something to tell you – something that will really interest you.'

Peter was a good friend and fellow educator. We'd never taught at the same school but I'd known him for the twenty years I'd been in Canada. He was originally from Liverpool and, as he often claimed, if you come from Liverpool a sense of humour is compulsory. But as well as a sense of humour he had the gift of the gab, which I had found useful on more than one awkward occasion. This was his honest inheritance from Irish ancestry. There was no doubt at all that his ancestors had enthusiastically kissed the blarney stone many times over!

Over a beer, I told Peter about my incredible balloon experience in the Yorkshire Dales. Like most people, of course, he was unfamiliar with the sport and he had a few erroneous assumptions about the details. He was particularly surprised to hear about the peace and tranquillity of a balloon flight and the leisurely sightseeing possibilities.

'I thought you'd be blown to bits up there!' he said, taken aback. 'I only ever had the one flight in an ultralight plane and I got practically blown out of the sky. I thought balloons would be pretty much the same.'

'No, no.' I assured him. 'This is completely different from ultralights. Balloons fly with the wind and at the same speed. The effect is like no wind at all. You could light a match and the flame would stand up straight, not even flickering, because the whole balloon becomes part of the moving air mass.'

Peter was quite intrigued and interested in the possibilities. 'I don't mind doing some training with you,' he said after hearing my story, 'but what about the cost?'

'It's not cheap,' I had to admit, 'and if you really get into it, get some training, buy a balloon and fly on a regular basis, it can be a pretty expensive sport. But there are ways around that. There are ways of covering your costs.'

'Such as?'

'Well, we could operate as a business and take paying passengers. It would be amazing fun, and we should be able to recoup our investment. The income from passengers would pay the ongoing expenses. Just think about it! After a stressful week at school what could be more relaxing than taking off for blue yonder on a Saturday morning with interesting people? Can't you just see us floating over the southern Ontario countryside in a beautiful hot-air balloon?'

Several beers later we had decided that we would at least check out any balloon companies within easy driving range of Toronto to see what was involved. I had already checked the Yellow Pages and I knew there were three companies within twenty miles or so. I agreed to contact them for some basic information. But the immediate problem was that we were both imminently due back at school. The whole idea would have to be put on hold for three or four weeks, and that would be awfully frustrating to say the least.

Over the following three weeks my days, evenings and weekends were fully occupied with the new job. I discovered that all the rumours about my new school were well founded. There were many needy children and families in the school community and I spent a lot of time working with staff to address the many pressing problems. For a while I had no time to think about balloons, but by mid-September things had settled down considerably, and one Saturday afternoon I put my mind to the task of obtaining some basic information.

I talked first with a remarkable balloonist in Newmarket called Helgi Sveinsson. He had an interesting Scandinavian accent but he told me that before coming to Canada he had been a balloon pilot in England for several years, and he actually knew Brian Turner.

'You know Brian?' I said incredulously.

'Sure I do! Brian and I flew together in several ballooning competitions. I knew his father; he was a balloonist too.'

That was quite a coincidence and we talked about Brian, about the Dales and about the uniquely beautiful English countryside that was so ideal for ballooning. Helgi explained that he was now involved in designing new experimental balloons with unusual shapes, but didn't do any training or teaching himself. The only flying he did was for his own satisfaction, though he did take out an occasional passenger flight.

Helgi finally suggested that if we were really interested in pilot training, we should contact a company called Canadian Balloon Highlights located in Goville, a small village north-east of Toronto. He was sure that they would be able to help.

I followed this advice immediately. The owner and operator of Canadian Balloon Highlights turned out to be a businessman by the name of Alan Crossland. I explained to him that Peter and I were interested in training as balloon pilots and we needed to talk to someone who could help us get qualified and licensed within a reasonable period of time.

'Are you intending to buy a balloon, then?' Alan asked, obviously seeing the potential for a sale.

'That's the general idea,' I told him, 'but we'll need some help and advice about what we should be looking for. We don't really know anything about hot-air balloons.'

'We're agents for Aerostar Balloons, mostly for business advertising purposes, but I'm sure we can help you with training, especially if you intend to buy a balloon from us.' He was friendly and helpful and I felt encouraged to discuss our project with him.

Over the course of my conversation with Alan I discovered that he was a keen balloon pilot and instructor himself. He had four full-time balloon pilots who worked for him, though they were frequently dispatched to various parts of the country on advertising contracts.

The main concern of Alan's business seemed to be advertising for big companies, using hot-air balloons as giant billboards in the sky and flying them under contract across Canada and the United States. However, he did have two pilots with instructor rating, and he had a smaller balloon that would be ideal for training. This balloon, he explained, was for sale, and we might be interested in buying it once we were licensed to fly. He suggested that we meet the following Wednesday evening to discuss possible plans for training.

This was very encouraging, and I could see that we might be able to get things moving faster than I had first thought. I finally had some positive information for Peter. I needed to keep him interested and involved because he had an awful tendency to flit from one interest to another without seeing anything to completion. I didn't want that to happen with the balloons.

'OK, we have a meeting set up to discuss training,' I told Peter when I called him later that day. 'How are you fixed for Wednesday evening?'

'It should be fine,' he said, happy to hear that we were making some progress. 'What have you worked out?'

I told him about my conversation with Helgi Sveinsson and how he had recommended Canadian Balloon Highlights as a good possibility.

'Alan Crossland seems like a good guy to deal with,' I told him enthusiastically. 'We should be able to get trained and buy a balloon all through the one company.' We agreed to drive up to Goville together on the following Wednesday evening to see what we could arrange with Alan Crossland.

Goville is a quiet, peaceful village, and it turned out that Alan lived on a ten-acre farm, three or four miles from town. He operated his business from the same location, an ideal set-up considering the amount of space needed for balloons and chase vehicles and the number of people who must inevitably come back and forth every day.

The house itself lay at the end of a long, winding driveway darkened by huge, overhanging trees. Trucks, trailers and private cars seemed to be parked everywhere. Two or three bikes leaned against a tumbledown barn in a heavily wooded section beside the two-story farmhouse. Through the open barn doors we could see several balloon baskets, assorted burners, and the large, green canvas bags that contained the balloon envelopes. We had come to the right place.

The front door opened even before we reached it, and a loud friendly voice, reminiscent of Brian Turner's booming vocals, greeted us. The voice belonged to a fairly heavy set man, perhaps thirty-five years old, with a friendly, smiling face. 'Come on in, guys! I'm Alan Crossland. We've been waiting for you.' He shook our hands as we reached the door. 'Go right through. Some of the guys are here after their afternoon flights.'

The narrow hallway led us directly into an unusually large kitchen. Four tired-looking men sat casually playing cards at the kitchen table, each with an open beer bottle in front of him. As Peter and I entered they turned to greet us, scraping their chairs noisily on the hardwood floor. Alan followed us in. 'Here's the two guys I told you about,' he announced, nudging us towards the group. 'Jon and Peter.'

'Hi! I'm Jon,' I said cheerily, extending my hand to the man on the nearest chair. He stood up immediately, grasping my hand in a firm grip. 'Bill Bauer,' he said, smiling. 'This is Kieran Rowan, a fellow pilot, and John and Matthew here are chasers. They've been crewing for us this afternoon.'

Peter introduced himself and shook their hands in turn. 'So this is how balloonists spend their spare time,' he joked. 'Playing cards and drinking beer!' They smiled weakly, not quite knowing what to make of Peter's unconventional approach to perfect strangers.

Alan offered us a beer, which we gratefully accepted, and for the next twenty minutes we chatted and socialized with the friendly group. I mentioned that I was an experienced ultralight pilot, and Alan was immediately interested. 'That's something I'd really like to try,' he said. 'Trouble is, I've got no time. I'm too busy with my balloons.'

'I've given up flying ultralight planes,' I explained. 'I've seen too many accidents. Besides, it's a bit of a lonely sport. I want something that's a bit more sociable.'

Eventually, Alan turned the conversation to the matter of balloon pilot training. 'We were thinking that Bill here could start you off as soon as you get your aviation medicals done,' he said, licking his thumb as he paged through a sheaf of printed papers. He looked up. 'Have you had a medical yet?'

'What's that all about,' Peter asked. 'What kind of medical?'

'You'll have to get signed off by a doctor who's approved for aviation medicals. I'll give you a name and number to call. It's no big deal; you can make an appointment.' Alan handed me a business card with the required information.

'You'll need logbooks,' he went on. 'You can get them at Oshawa municipal airport for about $20 or so. Get them before your first flight, because you'll have to record every bit of training you do. You'll need that to get licensed. You'll have to write the Air Regulations exam as soon as possible too.'

Peter took a long drink from his beer bottle. 'What about cost?' he asked. 'What do we do about payment?' I knew this would be an important matter for Peter. He was by no means short of funds, but as he'd told me many times before, when you come from Liverpool, every penny counts!

Alan was surprisingly vague on the question of payment. 'We can talk about it,' he said nonchalantly. 'Some people pay a deposit up front; some wait 'til they've done some training. It doesn't really matter. We're quite flexible.'

Who could argue with that? We said no more about it.

It was decided that Bill would take us on an orientation flight at the end of the following week, provided we passed our aviation medicals before then. The idea was to show us what flying a balloon is all about – inflation, level flying, landing, chasing and pack up. After that we could decide if we wanted to continue training or call it quits.

I was quite pleased with this agreement. We seemed to have stated our needs very clearly, and Alan Crossland had been extremely helpful and cooperative. 'That sounds great,' I said. 'I'm glad we could reach an agreement so quickly.'

'No problem,' said Alan as we stood up, preparing to leave. 'I'll be in touch, or Bill can call you. We've got your phone numbers. Good luck on your first flight.'

As we drove out along the dark driveway I felt immensely satisfied. This was really happening now. I had taken the first step to becoming a hot-air balloon pilot, and things were moving along. I got the feeling that Peter was less enthused than I. He had greatly enjoyed socializing over a beer or two with interesting people; that was his style. As for ballooning, it seemed he could take it or leave it. But for now, at least, he was going along with the plans we had made, and he was genuinely looking forward to his first flight.

A lot happened over the following ten days. Peter and I managed to make arrangements for aviation medicals and we both passed with flying colours. Alan Crossland had been right. It was no big deal, though a large amount of paper work was involved, and the physical exam itself seemed to take an inordinately long time. Because we were over forty, we were told we would have to have a medical exam every year, as long as we were flying.

Bill Bauer called the following week to see how things were shaping up.

'Are you all set for the weekend?' he asked.

'Absolutely! The medicals are done, and we have new logbooks.'

'Good,' he said. 'We'll be flying on Saturday morning, weather permitting. All being well, we can take off from here, Alan's place.'

'Well the weather forecast looks fine for Saturday,' I said hopefully.

'We don't go by the general forecast. I'll have to call aviation weather on the morning of the flight,' Bill explained. 'They'll give me the directions and speeds of winds aloft then I can make a decision on whether to fly or not, and we'll have an idea of where we'll be going. Calm winds are what we're looking for.'

I knew all that, but I feigned ignorance. I had been used to flying early morning in my ultralight plane, and I understood the importance of calm winds and cooperative weather.

'So what time will we be meeting?' I asked.

'You should be up here by six o'clock.'

'Six o'clock! Peter will die when he hears that.'

Bill laughed. 'He'd better get used to it. It's more like four-thirty in the summer months. No one flies balloons during the day because of the high thermals and wind sheers.' We left it at that. Bill would call at 5 a.m. on Saturday morning if the flight was on.

I gave Peter a call and explained the arrangements. As I had predicted, he was surprised about the early meeting, but we agreed to travel up to Goville together, once I had the OK from Bill.

We were finally on the point of taking the first step towards being qualified balloon pilots. All we had to do now was wait.

III
TESTY TRAINERS AND UNSCHEDULED FLIGHTS

I woke up with a start. The phone was ringing by the bedside arousing me from a shallow sleep. Naomi groaned and turned over as I reached out to answer. With a voice that didn't sound much like my own, I spoke into the phone.

'Hello!'

'Jon?'

'Yep.'

'It's Bill. We're on. Weather sounds great – calm surface winds; about seven degrees at the moment. Are you all set?'

'Absolutely! We're all set to go.'

'Great. I'll see you about six o'clock then at Alan's place.'

'We'll be there. See you soon.'

I was suddenly wide awake. I stumbled out of bed and called Peter from the basement phone to confirm everything was a go; then I washed and dressed in record time. No time to eat. We could do that later – maybe just an apple to nibble on for now.

I remembered my hot-air balloon flight in England and how I wished I'd worn proper boots. No mistake this time. I dressed warmly and wore sturdy footgear that I'd used when I was flying ultralight planes.

I stood outside in the early morning cool air, waiting for Peter to arrive and hoping he'd be able to get ready in time. I didn't want to be late for our first training session. I was relieved when I saw his car appear at the corner of the street.

'This is an ungodly hour for me,' Peter announced, yawning sleepily as he pulled onto my driveway. 'Good job I live so close.'

'Don't complain,' I told him, hopping into the passenger seat. 'It's almost six o'clock. We've got to get out of here.'

It was 6.20 by the time we reached Goville in the early morning light. Bill was leaning on the side of a smart-looking green Ford truck as we reached the end of Alan's driveway, arms folded and looking a bit impatient. 'Come on, guys,' he said with half a smile. 'The sun waits for no one.'

As we climbed out of Peter's battered car, two women came from behind the truck, shivering slightly in the cold air, each of them holding their collars up close to their necks. Though one was much older than the other, there was a striking resemblance between them.

'This is my girlfriend, Linda,' Bill said, putting his arm around the younger one, a pretty young woman in her mid-twenties, all dressed up in denim. 'She chases for all my flights – the best chaser I've ever had.'

'So you chase Bill?' Peter said, looking at her with a mischievous grin. 'I thought it would have been the other way round.'

I noticed a pained expression on the older woman's face as she raised her eyes to the sky and sighed deeply.

'And this is Betty, Linda's mother.' Bill turned his attention to the plump, middle-aged woman beside him. 'Linda's been wanting to arrange a flight for her mum for some time now, and I thought today would be a good opportunity, seeing as the winds are so calm.'

We dutifully shook their hands and exchanged a few pleasantries about the fine morning and the flight we were about to undertake. Betty seemed to be unsuitably dressed for ballooning, with her dress pants, smart jacket, and flimsy black shoes, though she seemed eager enough to take to the skies.

I felt somewhat annoyed inside. I didn't express my feelings, but I thought to myself, if this is a training flight, why are we taking a passenger? And why this particular passenger who seemed such an unlikely candidate for a balloon trip?

'Winds are from the south-west this morning,' Bill announced cheerfully as he opened the truck's narrow rear doors for us to squeeze in. Linda had quickly parked herself in the passenger seat upfront, leaving Peter and me to contend with Betty's awkward physique on the tiny back seat. We squeezed her in between us, much to Peter's amusement.

'We'll be taking off from the bottom field. I've just launched a piball and the upper winds still seem to be coming from the south-west. There's no wind to speak of at surface level, and they're quoting fifteen knots at 3000 feet. Perfect morning, really. We should travel ten miles or more.'

'What's a piball?' I enquired, intrigued by this new piece of information.

'Oh, we use a small helium-filled balloon. We send it off to test wind direction and speed at higher levels. Wind direction can be quite different a couple of hundred feet up. The piball tells us more or less which way we'll be going.'

Bill carefully manoeuvred the truck between the tall trees along a narrow pathway, obviously intended for pedestrians. As we emerged from the woods behind the farmhouse we pulled into a large field covered in tall weeds and grass. Beyond that was a magnificent view of rolling countryside. Distant silos and barns glittered in the sun, now gently lifting above the horizon. I felt a thrill of excitement as I anticipated a gentle flight into that wonderful, pastoral scene.

Selecting a spot that seemed to be almost exactly in the middle of the field, Bill stopped the truck in an area where the grass and weeds were well trodden down, suggesting that it was a regular launch site for Alan's balloons. 'This should be fine,' he said. 'Let's unload.'

The equipment was snugly packed and covered on the truck's steel flatbed, which could barely contain it. The basket, about the same size as Brian Turner's, though of a distinctly different style, took up most of the space; the burners, fan and the balloon envelope in its sturdy canvas bag had all been squeezed around it. As the three of us men strained to pull the heavy basket to the ground, Betty eyed it with some suspicion.

'Are we going up in that?' she asked apprehensively. 'I thought they were much bigger than that!'

'Don't worry, Mum,' Linda reassured her. 'It will seem much bigger once it's attached to the balloon. Everyone thinks the basket's too small the first time they see it.'

Peter looked over and smiled at her as Bill and I began to tug on the packed balloon. 'Is this your first flight, then?' he asked in a tone one might have expected from a professional balloonist. 'You'll be just fine. There's nothing to it really, especially on such a calm morning.' Betty, surprisingly reassured, didn't notice the wide-eyed expression on Bill's face as he quickly glanced at me. She stood a safe distance away and watched with folded arms, occasionally biting her lower lip, while we continued to work together under Bill's direction.

We attached the burners to the basket, using sturdy uprights from the corners for support. Bill tested each burner, causing both Peter and Betty to recoil in astonishment. I laughed smugly, remembering my first reaction to propane burners in Grassington. Betty covered her ears. 'My God!' she exclaimed in a tone of annoyance and complaint. 'That sounds like a dragon from hell!'

Bill explained every move as we dragged out the balloon from its bag. He showed us how to correctly hook the envelope to the karabiners on the burner frame, now attached to the basket as it lay on its side, and how to set up the fan in the correct position for the cold inflation. He then clearly demonstrated how the assisting crew should hold the mouth of the envelope wide open. I'd been a mere passenger on my first flight in England, but now I was a pilot in training and I felt very content with that.

Linda took care of the crown line while Peter and I held the mouth open and we watched in wonder as the balloon envelope magically transformed itself into an enormous marquee. I could see the look of amazement on Peter's face. He was obviously surprised and impressed.

Eventually, the balloon was sufficiently inflated with cold air from the fan, and Bill relit the pilot lights, ready to complete inflation with heat supplied by the powerful double burners. After a few long, deafening blasts, the balloon swayed and tugged against us as it struggled to rise.

'Here she comes!' Our instructor adjusted his position as the balloon came up, burning intermittently and swaying a little with the rising basket. 'Hold me down,' he yelled. 'One on each side of the basket. Keep your feet firmly on the ground.' Peter and I complied with his request, placing our collective weight on the basket, while Linda hurried towards us with the crown line, attaching it firmly to a karabiner. I noticed that this balloon had no scoop – just a large fireproof skirt that fell naturally around the mouth.

Betty looked quite bewildered in this flurry of last-minute activity, but Bill motioned her to approach the basket, and with some help from Peter, she clambered in. 'OK, guys,' he said. 'Climb in one at a time. Linda, take the strain.'

'I've got you,' she said calmly, obviously well used to the routine.

Betty clung tightly to one of the padded uprights while Peter and I found appropriate places at the sides of the basket. Bill continued to blast with short, frequent bursts of heat until Linda checked the buoyancy by partly removing her weight. 'You've got lift, Bill,' she informed him. 'Ready when you are.'

As Linda stepped back the balloon rose from the ground and slowly moved away from her, gently skimming the tops of the tall weeds across the full length of the field. Only when we reached the country lane beyond did we start to rise gently into the sky. We looked back to see Linda already pulling the fan onto the back of the truck and preparing for her chase. It would be considerably easier for her, I thought, on the straight roads of southern Ontario. Unlike Dave, she wouldn't have to cope with the winding country roads of the Yorkshire Dales.

Once we reached 1000 feet, Bill was settled and ready to explain his every move. 'Always have your radio set up where you can easily access it,' he told us, 'and as soon as you are settled, check it out with the chaser. You have to make sure it works when you need it.'

He took the microphone from its support on one of the padded uprights and officiously spoke into it. 'Aerostar to Ford! Checking communication.'

'I hear you loud and clear,' came Linda's casual voice in reply. 'Over.'

'Ten-Four!'

Over the next hour Bill skilfully controlled the balloon in its gentle voyage. It was a magnificent flight over beautiful countryside, farmland and forest. Lake Scugog was clearly visible ahead of us towards the north-east, glittering and shimmering in the morning sun and surrounded by breathtaking green pasture and scattered woods. Our instructor showed us how to change direction by increasing or decreasing altitude, taking extra care to make sure we understood how the burner's valve lever worked.

'The first thing to learn is how to maintain a steady flight path,' he explained. 'The balloon will fall as it naturally cools, so you have to anticipate that. Try to avoid a roller-coaster flight. You have to learn how to fly straight by burning at the right time.'

The flight was peaceful and calm, and by the time Bill started looking for a landing spot, even Betty was relaxed and content, now enjoying the beautiful scenery of Scugog county and the sheer thrill of flying in a balloon.

'We're landing in about fifteen minutes,' Bill announced into his radio.

'I've got you in sight,' came the reply.

We gradually approached some unoccupied pasture ahead, descending smoothly and accurately. It was a gentle landing. Bill touched down in a large field bordered by a sturdy, wooden fence, obviously constructed to keep large farm animals inside. With hardly a bounce at all in the calm air, the balloon rested gently on the ground about twenty feet from the edge of the field. Bill kept the envelope inflated with an occasional short burst of the burners, waiting for his chaser to arrive.

'Are you with us, Linda?' he called into his microphone.

'I've spoken to the landowner. There's no access to the field you're in; he's sent me into the field next door.'

Even as she spoke, Linda drove towards us on the other side of the fence. She stopped the truck a few feet away and jumped out, slamming the door behind her. 'What do you want to do, Bill?' She climbed on the fence, peering over at us with an enormous grin on her face, enjoying the predicament Bill found himself in.

'No big deal,' he said defiantly. 'We'll lift the balloon over the fence to your side.'

This should be an interesting learning experience, I thought, as Bill gently feathered the burners. How do you lift an enormous four-storey-tall giant over an eight-foot fence?

Bill had obviously done this before. He had it all worked out and confidently gave his directions. 'Peter, can you slowly get out of the basket now. Climb over the fence to help Linda. Jon, you get out after him as the balloon cools, but hang on to the basket. You'll have to drag us closer to the fence. Betty can stay in the basket with me for the lift over.' I got the distinct idea that Bill didn't want to deal with the daunting task of helping Betty climb the fence!

We followed the directions exactly, and Bill gently feathered the burners to gradually produce some lift. The basket rose two feet from the ground. Pulling and tugging with all my strength on the external rope handles, I tried to manoeuvre the balloon towards the fence. It was impossible. I was unable to make any progress at all by myself. The balloon was simply too heavy for one man.

Bill looked a little frustrated, as if to say someone stronger could have moved it with no problem. 'Never mind,' he said patiently. 'I'll come back down to ground level. The two of us together should be able to shift it.'

He allowed the balloon to sink and settle once more into the short grass. As the envelope cooled, he carefully climbed out of the basket, leaving Betty with a look of alarm on her flushed face. 'Don't worry,' he told her, seeing her apprehension. 'I need you to help me.' She reluctantly accepted this.

Bill grabbed the handles on one side of the basket while I positioned myself on the other. 'OK, Betty,' he said. 'Pump a little heat into the balloon to give us a bit of a lift over the fence. Just pull back on the valve-control handle above your head.'

'This one?' she asked, gingerly grabbing the handle.

'That's it. Just a little gentle heat.'

Betty's shaking hand nervously grasped the valve lever. Having no clue how to feather a propane burner, she firmly pulled it open to its full extent. With a deafening roar, the powerful blast sent enormous amounts of heat back into the balloon, giving Betty such a shock that she was unable to let go.

'My God!' Bill yelled at the top of his lungs. 'Turn it off!' But it was too late. With the burners still going at full blast the basket was torn out of our hands and Betty sailed off into the blue sky. 'Let go of the handle! Turn it off!' Bill was frantic, but to his great relief the burners suddenly stopped as Betty released her grip.

All was silent from above now as the balloon majestically climbed into the sky with its unwilling passenger. Fortunately, there was virtually no wind and the balloon hung over the field, barely moving from its position directly above our heads. As we helplessly gazed upward, Betty's worried face appeared over the side of the basket two hundred feet above us.

'The red line!' Bill yelled hysterically, his hands cupped to his mouth. 'Pull on the red rope!'

Betty evidently understood Bill's instruction for, with an almighty heave on the red deflation line, she ripped out the parachute top in one fell swoop and came crashing down to earth – on the other side of the fence!

Bill was beside himself. We dashed to the fence and clambered over with Olympic-style precision, surely beating any record that had ever been set. So hard was the landing that the balloon had covered the entire basket, hiding the terrified woman inside. Peter and Linda were already there, frantically tugging at the balloon fabric in an attempt to pull it away from around the basket that was still standing upright in the soft earth. As Bill and I joined them, Linda reached in and turned off the pilot lights, and then with one last sweeping pull she exposed her mother to fresh air once again. 'Mum!' she gasped. 'Are you OK?'

There was no response from Betty – just a blank, wide-eyed stare. Fortunately she was not injured, but the shock of her unscheduled aeronautic experience left her temporarily speechless. Linda helped her into the truck and gave her a bottle of water to sip on, and she sat there quietly contemplating the joys of hot-air ballooning while the rest of us packed up all the equipment and loaded the truck.

'Never allow a passenger to stay in the basket alone,' Bill advised us solemnly as we swung the heavy bag onto the back of the chase vehicle. 'As trainee pilots, if you learn one thing from today's flight that would be it. I made a serious error of judgement today, and all I can say is don't do what I do – do what I say.'

Peter and I stole a furtive tight-lipped glance at each other. I was afraid Peter was going to make some ill-advised humorous remark about Bill's technique for jumping fences, trivializing what had just happened to Betty, but seeing the look of embarrassment on Bill's face, he decided not to bother.

As we drove away Betty seemed to recover from her ordeal and she began to see the funny side of it. She was again squeezed between Peter and me in the narrow back seat of the truck and I noticed a faint smile appearing on her still flushed face. 'Wait till I tell my friends about this,' she chuckled. 'They thought I was nuts to go in a balloon anyway, but this will really make their day.'

Betty's lighter approach to the situation gave Peter the opening he wanted. He gave her a gentle nudge with his elbow and laughed out loud. 'Look at it this way,' he beamed with his Blarney smile. 'Jon and I were here for pilot training, but you're the one who got to do your first solo!'

Bill was strangely silent as he drove us all back to base.

IV
COWS, FENCES AND ANGRY FARMERS

'Don't do what I do – do what I say!' said Bill with a slight look of embarrassment. He grinned immediately, indicating that he was aware he had just made another bad mistake. He had let the balloon fall too close to a field full of cows. When he blasted the burners to gain some altitude it was too late; the herd panicked and scattered in all directions.

'We all make mistakes in this business,' he went on. 'It's part of the learning process. Even instructors have to keep on learning. I expect you two will make lots of mistakes before you get licensed.'

I glanced at Peter with a bemused expression. We were both experienced teachers and we didn't need any instruction about the learning process. We also knew that Bill had just made another serious error of judgement and he was trying to explain it away. We both knew that bothering livestock was a serious matter, and it could lead to legitimate complaints by local farmers.

'I guess you can't always judge the distances accurately enough to burn at exactly the right time,' I offered by way of excuse.

'I got too busy talking,' Bill explained. 'I should have seen that cow field long before we reached it, and I should have got some altitude to keep us well above it. The cows do get used to the blast of the burners, but this time we were just too close.'

The balloon was still rising after Bill's input of burner heat. The view was magnificent. We had again taken off from Goville, but this time we were heading north-west towards Lake Simcoe. Farms and fields, forest and glen, lakes and rivers, all stretched out before us in the early morning sunlight.

As the balloon sailed with the wind there was no sensation of breeze in our faces. Everything was calm and still, as if there were no wind at all. I thought of the pictures I had seen in books with balloons hurtling along like an open-cockpit biplane, flags flapping in the breeze and the pilot's hair and scarf trailing behind. So unrealistic, I thought; balloon flying is so peaceful and calm. As I had told Peter before, you could light a match and the flame would stand upright with barely a flicker.

'We're over two thousand feet already,' Peter announced, glancing at the altimeter strapped to one of the frame uprights. 'How high are we going on this flight, Bill?'

'Not much higher than this.'

Bill positioned himself in one of the corners of the wicker basket, which was impressively spacious for the three of us. 'I want each of you to take over the burners for a few minutes today. You can start learning level flying. Jon, you can go first.'

This was our second flight with Bill. Peter and I were hopeful that we could become hot-air balloon pilots in a fairly short time under his instruction, so we were eager to get on with some actual hands-on experience. I had been looking forward to using the burners. Licensing regulations required a minimum of twenty hours of burner time, and all the other instruction we were receiving, though absolutely essential and useful, didn't go in our logbooks. Only burner time counted. Here was my first opportunity, and I eagerly complied with Bill's request.

'Great,' I said, confidently moving into position and grasping the trigger on one of the burners. 'What's the plan?'

'Just try and keep the balloon flying straight and level,' Bill explained. 'Try and anticipate a descent as the balloon cools and supply some heat from the burners to prevent it from doing so.'

This was much harder than it sounded. I kept burning too late, so the balloon was flying like a roller coaster instead of in a straight line. Bill kept his hand on the second burner, ready to blast if we started to fall too quickly. This gave me some added confidence, and before too long I started to get the hang of it.

'More cows ahead,' Peter observed suddenly from his position at the front of the basket.

I gave an extra long blast of heat to keep us rising. The higher altitude gave us a slight turn to the right, moving us away from the cow field. Bill seemed impressed.

'That worked,' he said. 'In general, that's the way to do it. Go higher for a right turn, and let the balloon fall to move to the left. There's no steering wheel in this thing, you know. Altitude control is all we've got.'

The rest of the flight went smoothly enough. Peter did his roller coaster flying, as I had done. He managed to get twenty minutes of burner time to my fifteen. Soon after that it was time to start looking for a place to land.

As student pilots we had to leave this manoeuvre to our instructor. Landing a balloon is the most difficult thing to learn, and that part of the training comes when just about everything else has been fairly well mastered.

'I've got control,' said Bill in his instructor voice.

'You've got control,' we answered, using the standard response he had taught us to make sure there was no confusion about who was doing the flying. Bill was pleased that we remembered this safety procedure, and he grinned as he took control of the burners.

'You're learning,' he chuckled. 'Now let me concentrate on this landing.'

The wind had picked up during the flight and we were moving along at about fifteen knots. The wind speed would be much less at surface level, of course, and I anticipated a fairly soft landing. We soon began to fall quite noticeably.

Over the next few minutes I saw a look of anxiety developing on Bill's face. The balloon was gradually losing altitude as the envelope cooled, though an occasional blast from the burners kept the descent under control. I could see thick forest less than half a mile ahead of us and I knew we would have to touch down before we reached the trees.

Two or three open meadows lay straight ahead. These would have made perfect landing sites, but we were gradually moving to the left as we dropped below one thousand, then five hundred feet. Suddenly there was another large meadow in our flight path with thick forest behind it. We were committed to land. Unfortunately the field was full of cows.

'Shute!' said Bill, grasping the red deflation line with one hand while feathering the burners with the other. 'I've got no choice. I have to land in the cows.'

We all knew that this meant plenty of trouble. Dairy farmers hated balloons, and who could blame them? The sound of the powerful propane burners was terrifying to cattle, and if they were not used to balloons, anything could happen. I came to realize that even with the best of intentions and utmost care, any balloonist could find himself in this situation. Bill was mortified at being faced with such a precarious landing during a training session. He stared fixedly ahead, biting his lower lip and obviously feeling some stress.

As the balloon approached the field the surface winds were relatively calm, perhaps five knots, and this enabled our nervous instructor to at least do a stand-up landing.

'Hang on to those safety handles,' he murmured, sweat now visible on his brow. 'We are touching down – right here.'

Cows were running in all directions as the balloon gently touched down in the meadow. After one or two short bounces the basket settled in the grass. We could see the terrified cattle crowding one another into the fence at the far corner of the field, some of them desperately trying to climb over. They were making a dreadful noise too - enough to scare the living daylights out of anyone within half a mile.

Bill detached the crown line from its place on the karabiner. 'Can you take care of this?' he said, handing the end of the long stabilizing rope to Peter. 'Make sure there's no lift as you climb out of the basket; you may need to hang on for a minute. Pull the envelope down as quick as you can while Jon and I try and deflate from this end.'

As the envelope gradually cooled I climbed out of the basket. Peter was already using the crown line to pull the top of the balloon to the ground, and Bill used the deflation line to pull the top out from the inside. The basket slowly tipped and we were ready to start working our way along the balloon to squeeze out the air inside.

After a few minutes the cattle seemed to calm down considerably, obviously becoming used to our presence in the field. I glanced over at the gate some three hundred yards behind us and was relieved to see the chase vehicle gently bouncing its way through on the rough ground.

'Here's Linda!' I exclaimed. 'Thank goodness she stayed with us at the end. It looks like she had straightforward access to the field, anyway.'

Bill stood up straight, his eyes squinting over his sunglasses and his hands firmly on his hips. 'She's got company, though. See the tough looking character behind the truck? It looks like a woman – with a shotgun over her shoulder.'

The cows were rapidly losing interest in the balloon. Some had gone back to grazing. Others were curiously observing the proceedings from a safe distance. We could see the angry owner closing and chaining the metal gate while Linda drove the truck slowly across the field.

'Trouble!' she announced through the open window as she reached us. 'Big trouble, I'd say. This lady is the landowner, apparently, and she's already given me more than an earful.'

By now the balloon was almost totally deflated. Bill took a few slow steps in the direction of the gate and then stopped in his tracks with his hands in his pockets. He seemed to be nervously wondering how he was going to deal with the situation.

As I unhooked the last karabiner on the burner frame and pulled the basket upright, Peter made his way to my side. 'This should be our first lesson on how to deal with an angry farmer,' he said mischievously, leaning on the green suede trim of the basket, 'but I have a feeling we'll be the ones talking this lady down.'

'It's a good thing you have the gift of the gab, then.' I managed a forced grin.

Peter thrived on situations like this and I knew there was more than a good chance he'd soon be directly involved, and loving every minute of it.

The incensed farmer walked briskly towards us with the shotgun now held firmly in her tightly clenched fist. The other hand went purposefully to her left hip as she reached Bill, and an angry scowl was suddenly all too visible on her face. She was perhaps forty-five years old, no more than five and a half feet and solidly built, in keeping with her profession. Her well-worn jeans, red and black checked jacket, and baseball cap gave her a tough, masculine demeanour that seemed to say, 'Don't mess with me.'

'You're trespassing on private property!' she snapped before Bill could utter a single word.

'Yes, I know…'

'Forget the excuses,' she went on. 'That's my cattle you've terrorized with your blasted balloon and I want to know what you're going to do about it!'

'Well, I can only apologize,' Bill mumbled nervously. 'I certainly had no wish to …'

'Apologize! What the hell use is that? Half those cows will be calving in three months, and if there's any damage done I'll be suing you for compensation!'

I looked over at the herd, now grazing peacefully at the far end of the field. It seemed doubtful that any damage had been done, but I sympathized with this woman who was only defending her livelihood. I told myself that I would avoid causing such havoc to farmers and landowners when I completed my training and had a balloon of my own.

'Meanwhile,' bellowed the irate woman, 'I've locked the gates. You can all bugger off over the fence. Get off my land! I'm keeping the balloon and the truck till I know what the damage is.'

This news took Bill completely by surprise. He was astounded and seemed lost for words.

'Now just a minute,' he began, 'surely we can work something out …'

At this point Peter took over. With infinite confidence and charm he strode over to where the farmer and balloonist stood glaring at each other. Placing a friendly hand on Bill's shoulder, he looked at him with a wry smile.

'Bill,' he said, 'this lady's absolutely right. We are trespassing on her land and she has every right to complain. She's concerned about her cows, for heaven's sake.'

The woman seemed taken aback by these words of support, as if she had been expecting some violent protest on our part. She was momentarily stumped.

'I'm so sorry, ma'am,' Peter went on. 'We found ourselves in an impossible situation and we couldn't avoid landing here. I know that's no consolation to you; you've every right to be angry and upset. We're as concerned as you are about the cattle. I do hope we have done no damage. But by all means, keep the equipment as collateral if you think we have.'

Bill looked aghast. His mouth opened but no words came out.

The woman's voice was noticeably calmer, though still angry and upset. 'I'm just worried about losing my new calves,' she said. 'I've invested a lot of money in this enterprise, and you guys don't seem to give a damn.'

'Believe me, ma'am, we do care,' Peter explained sympathetically. 'And we want to make some kind of restitution for the inconvenience we've caused you. This balloon is worth about $40,000, so I imagine it will be enough. I assume you have a safe place to store it. Your insurance company should be able to cover it against damage for a few hundred dollars until the lawyers can sort everything out.'

The farmer's bluff was called and she quickly backed down.

'Well, I'm not saying I want to get into all that. Maybe you should just get the stuff off my land. But I am not opening that gate unless you can leave something of value as security. Once you leave here I've got no control.'

She was right, of course. But Peter was ready with his next line.

'Suppose we just give you all the money we have with us as a kind of landing fee? That will cover the nuisance factor and pay something for the inconvenience.'

The woman adjusted her cap and scratched her head. She pondered this idea for a few seconds and seemed mildly interested. 'How much will that be then?'

'Everything we've got.' Peter looked around and raised his eyebrows at us.

'Bill, how much cash have you got?'

Bill fished around in his pockets and pulled out a few bills. 'I've got $65,' he said, reluctantly handing it over to Peter.

'Jon, how about you?'

I had already produced the small amount of cash I had in my back pocket – two twenties and a ten. I handed it over, somewhat amused at this rather unusual rescue strategy.

'Linda?'

Searching through her purse, which she had left on the driver's seat in the truck, Linda produced $85, which she brought over to add to the collection. 'Grocery money,' she mumbled ruefully.

Peter carefully organized the bills into a neat bundle. After folding the cash he placed it firmly in the farmer's hand and nonchalantly announced, 'There! I don't have any cash on me myself, but that's $200. Sorry it can't be more, but like I said, it's all we have.'

The scowl on the woman's face turned to an expression of mild satisfaction. She knew quite well that although the cattle had been excited, no real damage was done. She had been angry at the unwanted intrusion and our seeming lack of care, but she had no real concerns about damage. The $200 seemed to cover the cost of inconvenience.

'Right, then,' she said. 'Get off my land and don't bother coming back.'

The woman marched off in the direction of the gate, stuffing the cash into the back pocket of her jeans as she went. The shotgun was pointed to the ground now and I couldn't help but wonder if it was really loaded. We watched her until she reached the large metal gate. She removed the padlocked chains and then disappeared in the direction of the small, tidy-looking farmhouse at the top of the gravel driveway. Peter turned and looked at us with a wide, triumphant grin.

'I suggest we pack up and get the heck out of here as fast as we can.'

We needed no further encouragement. Within a few minutes the balloon was safely packed into its large canvas bag, and the basket and burners loaded on to the back of the truck. We all piled into the chase vehicle, glad to be out of this mess and on our way home. Bill was quieter than usual, obviously pondering his reduced leadership role, and no doubt embarrassed that he had been forced to rely on his students to save the day.

As we slowly crossed the field we saw that the farmer had returned to chain and padlock the gate behind us. She stood glaring at us, holding it open for us to drive through. Peter, who was sitting in the front passenger seat, gave her a wide, charming grin as the truck rumbled its way out of the field. I noticed the faintest flicker of a smile cross the woman's work-lined face as we hurriedly drove away.

Once we were clear of the woman's property, Peter turned around and beamed at us all with his Blarney-stone smile. He held a wad of money in his hand.

'Breakfast anyone?' he said. 'It's on me!'

V
BURNT BOTTOMS AND DRAG LANDINGS

'You'll need to direct the blast towards the centre of the envelope. See the way the vent is nicely covered now as the balloon becomes more inflated. That will rise as you add some heat, but try and direct the flames to that same spot as she goes up.'

Bill explained the procedure clearly and patiently. He seemed to have recovered from the cow field experience and he was getting used to training Peter and me on a weekly basis. By mid-November we had done half a dozen successful flights, and we had managed to accumulate close to three hours of burner time each. We were becoming quite proficient at level flying. Now it was time to learn how to do a hot inflation and take-off.

'As you know, I haven't done this before,' I told my instructor with some trepidation as I climbed into the tipped basket. 'I don't want to mess up the inflation. And, more importantly, I don't want to burn your balloon.'

'You'll be fine,' said Bill with a hint of impatience in his voice. 'How can you learn if you don't actually do the job yourself?'

That's true enough, I thought. Hands-on experience is what it's all about.

We had to give credit to Bill for his patience and endurance. Ballooning was clearly his passion, but we got the impression that he wasn't really keen on being an instructor. Teaching us must have been quite a pain for him too, considering that we were both teachers ourselves and knew a thing or two about good instruction. Bill didn't always reach the mark when it came to teaching, but he was a good, competent balloon pilot with a few hundred hours of flying time. He knew what he was doing.

'Get ready with those burners now,' he told me hurriedly. 'I want you to be ready to blast the hell out of them when I give the word.' In tense moments he always seemed to be preoccupied with the fear of something going wrong.

I settled myself into the basket and started to manoeuvre the burners into the right position. These double burners had the ability to blast out enormous amounts of heat in their ten-foot flames. We would need that heat once we were ready for the hot inflation, and I nervously placed my hands on the triggers, ready for action.

'I'm all set now,' I shouted over the noise of the fan. 'I'm ready when you are.'

There was still plenty of fabric to be pulled out from underneath. Peter and Bill worked their way around the balloon, pulling and tugging to make sure everything was fully extended before the hot inflation could start. Linda usually took care of the crown line, but today Bill was intent on giving us new jobs. I could see him becoming more anxious as the balloon got harder to control in the light breeze.

'OK, Peter, you grab the crown line today and see if you can stop her from rolling,' he barked.

Peter hurried to his position. He had seen Linda do this several times and he knew exactly what to do. 'I've got her,' he shouted back, holding down the top of the balloon with the long crown rope while he strained with the increasing resistance from the inflating fabric.

It was a crucial phase in the inflation process. The fan could complete the inflation up to a point, but the hot inflation had to start at exactly the right moment for satisfactory results. There was a tendency for the mouth of the balloon to close before sufficient heat could be blasted in, and this often meant starting over from scratch.

'Almost there!' Bill hollered as he joined his girlfriend at the mouth of the balloon. He looked over at me anxiously. 'Don't start until I give you the signal.'

The two of them grabbed the fabric around the mouth, creating a large opening for me. The fire-resistant skirt still lay scrunched up on the ground between the balloon and the basket. Bill looked at it with some annoyance and sighed, as if he had expected someone else to deal with it. He moved over between the burners and the mouth to smooth it out, raising his hand purposefully to make sure I restrained the heat while he made his last-minute adjustments.

I had been greatly looking forward to this stage of my training. I could feel my heart racing along as I anticipated this final phase in preparing the balloon for flight. It was my first unassisted hot inflation, and I relished the moment. I could feel my hands sweating inside the protective gloves that we all used when handling the burners.

'I'm all set to go!' I shouted above the fan's roar, anxious to get started.

'OK, we're going to hold the mouth open for you as wide as possible,' Bill yelled back. 'Aim for the centre! Direct some long blasts to the top, followed by some short ones until she comes up.'

Bill moved partway back to his position at the mouth, but suddenly something caught his attention. He still wasn't satisfied with the way the skirt was positioned on the ground, and in a flash he was back on his hands and knees, hurriedly pulling the material back and forth to make it lie flat on the ground. I only remember the vision of his workman's cleavage before my eyes a moment before. Then my nervous fingers found a mind of their own and pulled on both triggers. The ear-shattering blast of the burners could hardly drown out Bill's astonished howl.

'O my God!' he roared as he jumped out from the balloon's mouth, the seat of his jeans floating away in scorched pieces. 'What the hell are you doing, man?'

I couldn't believe what I had just done. Messing up my first hot inflation no longer seemed important or relevant. I had literally burned the pants off my instructor's backside. How would I ever live that down?

Bill looked at me with an incredulous expression, his mouth open but totally lost for words. He turned and walked away, vigorously rubbing his backside, which sent more scorched fabric into the morning breeze, much to Linda's stifled amusement.

'Bill,' I offered lamely, 'I'm so sorry.'

'Turn those damn burners off right now,' he whimpered over his shoulder. 'This flight's cancelled!'

~

The following week seemed to drag on. I was mortified at what had happened, and I was disappointed that my first take-off attempt had been such an abysmal failure. Things were not helped by Peter's bizarre jokes. 'Are we having another barbecue soon?' he asked when he called me mid-week. 'A nice bit of rump roast might be a good idea.'

'It's not funny,' I tried to tell him. 'Bill was really upset about it. He may not want to see us again.'

'Well Linda thought it was hilarious. Didn't you see her trying to swallow the giggles? They've probably split up over it by now.'

Bill was in the habit of calling me each Friday evening to speculate about Saturday's training session. I wondered if the call would come this week as usual, and if it did, what frame of mind he'd be in.

When the phone rang at the usual time my heart jumped, and I answered it with some apprehension, though I was careful not to show it.

'Hello!' I said, sounding full of confidence and self-assurance.

'Jon?'

'Yes, hello, Bill.'

'It's not Bill. It's Alan – Alan Crossland.'

That caught me by surprise. But Alan seemed to be his usual cheery self, and I felt relieved about that. I thought perhaps he might have been annoyed about the incident with the burners, but there was no mention of it. He simply explained that Bill wasn't going to be available for the weekend.

'As a matter of fact,' he explained, 'Bill's going out to Calgary for a few weeks to do some advertising for me on a new contract. Linda's going with him; they're quite excited about it.'

'Oh!' I exclaimed, surprised at this news. 'So I guess our training's off for now?'

'Well, no, you're fine for tomorrow. Kieran Rowan can take care of your training session this week. He'll be calling you later tonight once he gets an aviation weather report. After that I don't know. Kieran's due back in Quebec next week, so he won't be available either. We'll have to see how it goes.' I thanked Alan for the information and he rang off with a friendly goodnight.

Within the hour Kieran Rowan was on the phone to make arrangements for the following day's flight. We had only met Kieran the one time, when we first went to make arrangements with Alan two months previously. I remembered him as an outgoing, self-confident type, quite different to Bill, but obviously just as keen and competent.

'They're forecasting windy conditions for tomorrow morning,' he told me. 'I wouldn't take paying passengers, but it should be OK for a training session. How many hours have you got so far?'

'About three hours each,' I told him.

'That's not a lot, but if you're going to be pilots you'll have to learn how to deal with high winds. As long as surface winds are not over ten knots I think we should go, but I'll confirm with you tomorrow morning when I see what's going on.'

The early morning phone call confirmed that the flight was on. Peter and I met Kieran and his one-man crew about 6.30 at a popular launch site in Mount Albert, ten miles north of Alan's place. He greeted us heartily and showed genuine interest in our training so far and the progress we were making. John, the chaser, was a muscular young man who didn't have much to say to us, although we had met him before at Alan's farm. He seemed like a shy fellow, but his hefty build and six-foot-four frame made him particularly suitable for the job.

'I want to get moving,' Kieran said after engaging in a minimum of small talk. 'The morning forecast indicates surface winds are from the north at about 10 knots and upper winds 20 knots and higher. They're supposed to calm a little by mid-morning, but you never know. We'll be flying at the limits for sure. Ten knots is usually considered maximum.'

This was a new experience for us. We had only flown on calm days before, and the prospect of flying in windy conditions was quite exciting, though a bit daunting too. I was eager to learn all aspects of ballooning. This would be a good opportunity to fly in different weather conditions and with a different instructor.

'One of you can do the hot inflation and take-off,' Kieran said as we started unloading the truck. 'Who wants to do it?'

Peter grinned and nodded in my direction. 'Jon's particularly good at hot inflations. Mind you, he could use some more practice. Let him do it.' The joke was obviously lost on our new instructor.

'That's fine. You can take care of the fan and cold inflation while you're at it.'

We watched as the strapping young chaser single-handedly hauled first the packed balloon and then the basket off the back of the truck, dragging them away to a clear spot with a great deal of huffing and puffing.

'Big John will take care of the crown line this morning,' Kieran informed us, observing his assistant's heroic efforts with some amusement. 'With these windy conditions it's going to be harder to keep things under control, but he can handle it; he's well used to it.'

Between the four of us we prepared the balloon for flight, occasionally fighting the surface wind. As we spread out the envelope the breeze began to inflate it without the assistance of the fan, moving things along much faster than usual. Once I had started the inflation fan the balloon filled rapidly, and under Kieran's expert direction I was soon ready to make my second attempt at a hot inflation and take-off.

'This will be a bit trickier than what you're used to,' Kieran shouted over the fan's clatter as I climbed into the basket and positioned myself behind the burners. He held the mouth wide open, assisted by Peter on the other side, and as the balloon rolled gently from side to side in the light breeze, my instructor motioned to me to begin burning. 'Let's go!' he yelled. 'Give her all you've got!'

With Kieran's patient, competent approach to instruction, I felt much more at ease now, and although this inflation was under more difficult conditions, I was able to complete it with no problem. I blasted the flame towards the crown in short, powerful bursts, and in a surprisingly short time the balloon rose magnificently to its position over the basket.

My instructor immediately jumped in with me. 'Well done,' he exclaimed. 'That was a great inflation. Now let's do a great take-off.' The chaser held down the basket, Peter climbed in, and after a few last-minute safety checks we were ready to go.

A row of tall trees stood behind us and this gave us some shelter that I had not taken into account. As the balloon slowly rose above tree-top level I was aware of a marked increase in directional speed, and looking down to our launch site in the field below, I was taken aback at how quickly the chase vehicle and its driver were disappearing from view.

'We'll move at a good clip today,' said Kieran, seeing my surprise. 'We could easily travel twenty miles or more.' I thought I detected a faint note of angst in his voice, but I had found the successful launch so satisfying and exhilarating that I consciously dismissed any thoughts of anxiety.

As we gained altitude the balloon naturally shifted towards the south-west and our flight path took us in the direction of the town of Aurora and the countryside beyond. The flight was going well. I had been in control of the craft since take-off and I felt pleased with my performance and with the fact that my instructor was quite satisfied too.

'You've learned a lot; Bill's done a good job with you,' Kieran observed. 'That's good level flying you're doing there.' He peered over the side of the basket at the network of roads below. 'I don't see the truck down there. Big John's probably having trouble keeping up this morning.'

After about thirty minutes flying it was Peter's turn for some burner time. I was about to mention it, but Kieran spoke first.

'Look,' he said seriously, 'I think I'm going to cut this flight short. We're really moving now. That's Newmarket you can see ahead, which means we've travelled fifteen miles in half an hour. It's going to be a rough landing. And it'll only get worse as time goes by, so I think we'd better land as soon as we can.' He looked at me cautiously. 'Have you done a drag landing before?'

'I've never done any kind of landing. And we've only flown in calm conditions so far, so this will be something new.'

'That's fine. Let me take over, then. You'll have to hold on tight to those safety handles. This basket's going to tip once we hit the ground.'

Kieran explained to us that drag landings are quite normal and there was nothing to be concerned about. 'The basket will tip on contact with the ground if there's any significant wind,' he explained, 'but as long as everyone holds tight it will be fine. It's just the way balloons land.'

Over the next ten minutes I watched an expert prepare to land a balloon in windy conditions. Our instructor first of all contacted John in the chase vehicle to tell him we were coming down, and to his relief received instant acknowledgment. Now it was a question of gradually descending and choosing an appropriate landing site. As we lost altitude I realized how fast we were actually moving in relation to the ground, and I instinctively grasped one of the rope handles behind me. I noticed a strangely quiet Peter doing the same.

'We'll need a long field for this one,' Kieran murmured, looking ahead and crouching slightly as he gripped the red line and gently feathered the burners. He smiled. 'And the perfect field is coming up.'

I could see a long stretch of green about half a mile ahead, but it lay to the left of our flight path and I wondered if the balloon would veer sufficiently to allow us to land there. I needn't have worried. Like magic, the balloon slowly changed its flight path as we approached the ground so that at a hundred feet we were lined up for the perfect landing.

'Peter, grab this red line. When I give you the word, rip out that top as hard and as fast as you can.' Kieran's concentration was intense. He narrowed his eyes and grabbed a handle with one hand while feathering the burners with the other. The wind carried us forward at a furious rate, and suddenly we were three feet from the ground over short, manicured grass.

'Now!' Kieran yelled at the top of his lungs. 'Rip her out!'

Peter was ready. With all his might he pulled out the parachute top, furiously working his way along the deflation line until the top was completely open. Almost instantly, the basket hit the ground, tipped to its side and dragged along the ground like a speeding bullet. It was the ultimate in excitement and exhilaration. So this was a drag landing. I remembered Brian Turner wishing we could have had one on the Dales flight, and I realized why it was just a joke. Some passengers might not appreciate such an aggressive conclusion to their flight in a hot-air balloon.

'Wow! That was some landing, man.' Peter lay on his back with the red line still in his hand as the basket finally came to an abrupt halt. The envelope was completely deflated.

'That's the way it's done,' Kieran panted, now looking out of breath after his heroic efforts. He climbed out of the basket and Peter and I followed him, feeling both relieved and content with our new experience.

The three of us leaned on the basket and looked around at our surroundings. The grassy area we had landed on appeared far more extensive now. We were in a shallow valley, long and flat in the middle with sloping grassy banks on all sides. Tall trees bordered one edge of the valley, and we could see what appeared to be cultivated gardens on the other. A pathway ran through the trees. We assumed that some opulent residence lay on the other side.

'No sign of John, yet.' Kieran pulled out his microphone from inside the basket and attempted to make radio contact. There was no reply. 'He must be out of the truck. Let's start packing up this stuff.'

Twenty minutes later the balloon was safely stored back in its bag, the burners were dismantled, and we had everything ready to load. But no sign of our chaser. Suddenly, the sound of a car engine attracted our attention. We expected to see the chase vehicle but instead we were surprised to see a gleaming white Cadillac now stopped at the top of the pathway in the trees.

'That's John in the passenger seat.' Kieran took a few steps in the direction of the luxury car, hands on hips, and straining to see with narrowed eyes. 'What's going on?'

We looked at each other, mystified by this development and unsure about what to do. As we stared across at the Cadillac, it slowly backed and turned, then disappeared once more behind the trees. We could hear the engine, ever fainter as it moved away.

'Give it five minutes,' Kieran advised. 'I'm sure he'll be back.'

Sure enough, a few minutes later we heard the familiar sound of the chase vehicle and we were relieved to see it rolling into the field. Walking behind were two ominous looking dudes dressed in white jackets and black pants. Dark sunglasses added purposeful attitude to their poker-faced expressions, and they stopped, arms folded, at the end of the pathway, leaving John to drive alone towards us. His window was down as he stopped beside us, and he looked at us with bemused sarcasm.

'Do you realize where you've landed?' he said dryly. 'This is the Rodrigues estate!'

He climbed out of the truck with a slight grin on his face as he explained. 'This place is surrounded by high-level security – brick walls, electric fences, guard dogs, the lot. I didn't think they were going to let me in.'

I had heard about the Rodrigues family. They were of South American origin, enormously wealthy, and recently they'd been in the news because of alleged connections to organized crime. Nothing had been proved and no charges had been laid, but they were surrounded by mystery and intrigue.

'So what have they said?' Kieran looked rather concerned. 'Are we allowed to leave?'

'Oh, yeah! They want us to pack up and go. They'll escort us out.'

Everything was already packed, so it was just a matter of loading the truck. This was done in very short order, and we were quickly on our way. The white-coated dudes stood aside for us, poker-faced, as we drove through. I thought perhaps they had changed their minds about escorting us out, but as we emerged from the woods on the other side, another gentleman was waiting for us. He was a middle-aged, heavy-set man, poker-faced like the others and wearing the signature sunglasses. He also held a huge Doberman pincher on a very short, leather lead. He motioned silently as we slowly approached and indicated that we should follow him.

'The joys of ballooning! I feel like I'm in some weird movie.' Peter broke the tense silence in the truck and we all relaxed a little.

Our unwilling host led us along beautifully landscaped pathways, embellished with pink gravel and bordered with a variety of plants. An imposing stately home of regal quality stood back some distance from the manicured lawns, but apart from our guide, it seemed that no one was around.

Eventually, we reached the ten-foot tall wrought-iron gates, which were opened widely for us to pass through. Only Peter dared to wave goodbye, but his pert salutation was greeted with a brazen, stony face. As we drove away we heard the gates close behind us with a resounding clang.

Back in Mount Albert forty minutes later, Kieran signed our logbooks and chuckled about the morning's events. 'When you're a balloonist, anything can happen,' he told us with enthusiasm and pride. 'You've got it all to come.' He handed us our logbooks and shook our hands heartily. 'Good luck with your training, guys. I'm off to Quebec next week so I don't know if I'll see you again, but I've enjoyed flying with you today.'

The two of them drove off, leaving us alone. As we climbed into my Buick for the trip home, I realized for the first time that our future training was now on hold. No arrangements, tentative or otherwise, had been made for our next training session.

'So where do we go from here?' I asked Peter. 'What do we do now?'

'Well,' he said casually. 'I've enjoyed every minute of it. We've met some great people and it's been a lot of fun. We've had some great flights and now we've experienced the drag landing, too – what more could you want? I wouldn't mind really if Alan

Crossland never called us again. There are other things I want to do.'

I pondered this during the drive home. I was bound and determined to become a fully qualified hot-air balloon pilot, but it seemed to me there was a distinct possibility that from now on I'd be on my own.

VI
BALLOONING IN A WINTER WONDERLAND

We never heard from Alan Crossland again. As the weeks went by, I realized that our training with Canadian Balloon Highlights was over. Alan was too busy with his advertising business, and with lucrative contracts all over the country he wasn't about to waste his pilots' time training two duffers from Duffins Creek. Balloon pilots were too hard to come by, and unless there was a definite sale involved he couldn't afford to use them for training sessions that were relatively unprofitable. I knew that if I was serious about continuing my training I would have to find a new instructor who could take the time to involve me in a full, professional programme.

During my initial research at the end of the summer I'd noticed that the Yellow Pages listed a representative for Cameron Balloons under a company called Northern Balloon Adventures. They operated from Stoneville, a small town north of Toronto. This had attracted my attention at the time because I knew that Brian Turner's balloon was a Cameron, and during my flight in England I'd been impressed by the balloon's obvious quality and relative simplicity. The fact that the Cameron was British made appealed to me too, and it was reassuring to know that, according to their advertising, they sold more balloons worldwide than any other company. They obviously had an excellent support system in place and I wondered if they might provide instruction as well.

I tried to renew Peter's interest and suggested that we contact Northern Balloon Adventures for more information, but to no avail. He had enrolled in a squash programme at Duffins Creek Community Centre and now all his energy was directed towards playing his league games with a view to winning the upcoming tournament. 'Besides,' he said, 'isn't it getting a little cold for ballooning? It'll be Christmas in two weeks!'

I realized he was right. The Christmas holidays were upon us. Things were hectic at school too, with student reports due and preparations for an ambitious Christmas concert underway. It seemed best to forget about ballooning for the moment. I could always renew my efforts in the new year.

The holidays quickly passed and the cold Canadian winter soon set in. It was mid-January when I finally made contact with Northern Balloon Adventures. I'd never really thought about hot-air ballooning during the winter months, and I wasn't even sure anyone would be doing it. The temperature was at minus 20 degrees. Most sporty and active Canadians were involved in skiing, tobogganing and, of course, hockey, and here was I looking for balloon instruction. I didn't know whether I should feel uncommonly brave or utterly foolish. But the phone call I made that day put my mind at rest and placed my ballooning future firmly back on track.

It was all business from the start. I discovered that Northern Balloon Adventures was run by Simon Wills, an Englishman who represented the interests of Cameron Balloons in Canada. He spoke with an accent that made it clear he was from somewhere in the south, and I was immediately impressed by his professional approach and expert knowledge. I explained to him what had taken place so far, how we had begun training with Canadian Balloon Highlights and how the programme had ended so abruptly.

Simon listened sympathetically and assured me that he would be able to help. His business, he told me, was geared to passenger flights and sales. He was a fully qualified instructor and he was authorized to sign students off for pilot licences and instructor ratings for all free-flying balloons. It sounded perfect – exactly what I was looking for.

'I don't spend much time instructing,' Simon advised me. 'You'd have to commit yourself to buying a new balloon, otherwise it's not financially feasible for me to put in the amount of time needed. Besides, what's the use of getting your licence if you don't have a balloon to fly?'

I had to agree. 'I've every intention of buying a balloon,' I assured him. 'In fact, I plan to start my own company and run passenger flights myself.' I quickly realized the implication of what I had just said and hastily added, 'Not that I want to give you any unwanted competition.'

Simon laughed heartily. 'Not much danger of that! You'll need a lot of experience before you can take paying passengers.'

Over the rest of the lengthy telephone conversation, Simon Wills told me that he had three huge balloons that carried eight passengers each, and two smaller ones suitable for small groups or for pilot instruction. Winter flights were quite popular, he explained. Three or four pilots worked for him on a part-time basis, and he was consistently busy with passenger flights every weekend and during the week as well. He suggested that we meet as soon as possible to do a winter flight so he could assess my present skills and work out a suitable training plan. To my surprise and delight, he promised to complete my training before the summer. I'd be a qualified balloon pilot by the end of May.

~

The nitrogen cylinder scraped along the concrete floor making a nail-biting screech as Simon Wills pulled it closer to the basket. As I walked into the freezing detached garage I could see now that he was a tall, athletic-looking man, about thirty-six years old and appearing every bit as professional as he had sounded on the phone. He was dressed in a navy blue flying suit that seemed to have been specially designed for winter use, and his ears were covered with padded muffs that extended from his headgear.

He left the heavy cylinder and walked over to me when he saw me enter. 'Simon Wills. Glad you could make it,' he said, removing a glove and extending his hand with a welcoming smile. 'I'm just getting the propane fuel tanks ready for the flight.'

He continued talking as he returned to the task at hand. 'It's a pain having to pressurize these tanks,' he said with some frustration. 'But we'll be in real trouble if we don't do it on a day like this. It was minus 22 degrees last time I checked.'

He connected the nozzle to each of the four tanks in turn, carefully adjusting the pressure gauge each time. 'That should do it,' he said after much banging and clattering. The propane fuel tank hissed loudly as he unscrewed the brass connector.

It was a bitterly cold morning for ballooning and I felt like a padded Santa Claus in my layers of woollen sweaters. But I was excited and eager on this January day. I felt very fortunate that Simon had agreed to finish the training programme with me after things had fallen through with Canadian Balloon Highlights. This was the first time I had met him, of course, but already I felt very comfortable and confident with my new instructor.

'Propane doesn't have sufficient pressure in sub-zero temperatures,' he explained. 'But the nitrogen pressurizes the tank so we can fly more or less normally, no matter how cold it is.' He pulled the nitrogen tank away from the basket and his young assistant hurried to help.

'Paul will be chasing for us today,' Simon informed me, realizing that I had not been introduced to him. 'He's started his training with us, and I don't think I have ever had a more enthusiastic student. He's around here every spare minute he gets.'

I shook Paul's hand with a smile. 'Jon,' I said. 'I guess we'll be students together then. How long have you been training?'

'Oh, I've only just started; two hours burner time so far – and a whole lot of chasing.'

Paul was a good-looking young lad of about seventeen, but with his slight build and being dressed up for the cold weather, he looked more like a younger boy out for a morning of skating or tobogganing. I discovered later that Simon was training him as a balloon pilot in exchange for working as a chaser and general helper.

'If you can believe it,' I told him, 'I have about three hours of burner time, but I have never done any chasing at all.'

'That'll change,' Simon chipped in with a laugh. 'As far as I'm concerned, you can't be a pilot unless you are a darned good chaser first. I won't sign anyone off until they know every aspect of ballooning inside out – and that includes chasing.'

I'd discovered that Simon's reputation as a professional balloonist and instructor was impeccable, and I knew I was lucky to have him as my new trainer. I was sure I'd be a competent, knowledgeable and safe pilot by the time I finished my training under his guidance.

We loaded the basket and accessories onto the trailer that was already hitched to the chase vehicle. There was just about enough room left to squeeze the balloon behind and Simon and I easily swung it into place, pushing it down deep in the trailer. It seemed lighter than I had been used to, and Simon, seeing my look of surprise, explained.

'We're using the 65 today, seeing that there's only the two of us. It has an official payload of about 420 pounds but in this cold air it could lift much more. You'll probably find it quite small and easy to fly if you've been used to flying a Seven up to now.'

The truck engine started under protest in the sub-zero temperature, groaning and complaining until it finally caught. After allowing a minute or two to warm up, Paul drove us slowly off the driveway and made his way through the residential streets to the country roads beyond.

'Where are we launching from today?' I enquired, leaning forward from the rear seat and straining to read an obscure signpost.

'Mount Albert,' came the reply.

'Ah! Mount Albert. That's where we launched on my last flight in November.'

'It's a popular take-off spot. We might see someone else there, though I doubt it. I seem to be the only one flying in the winter this year.'

I was intrigued with the winter flying and eager to understand the implications. 'Don't you find it awfully cold up there?' I mean, minus 20 degrees...'

'Well, it's no colder than on the ground. In fact it feels a lot warmer because you don't feel the wind. As you know, there's no wind chill in a balloon. You just have to dress warmly, that's all.'

As we drove along the deserted country roads to our destination, Simon chatted about various aspects of training and the pros and cons of flying at different times of the year. 'Actually,' he said, 'winter is by far the best time to learn. There are no crops in the fields and all the animals are inside. You can land just about anywhere without annoying anyone. It's a great time to practice landing. Maybe we should try a few landings today.'

We were at the Mount Albert site within thirty minutes. The take-off site looked somewhat different to what I remembered as it was now covered in deep snow, and the trees on the north side were completely bare, giving less protection against the wind. That didn't matter today, however. The winds were totally calm at ground level.

The chase vehicle's heavy commercial tires had no difficulty coping with the powdery snow. Paul was obviously quite used to working with the truck and trailer and he quickly manoeuvred them into position so that unloading was easy and straightforward. Simon and I dragged out the envelope together and we soon had it attached to the basket as it lay on its side in the snow. I needed some help with the assembly as I was unfamiliar with the peculiarities of a Cameron.

'Right, then,' Simon said cheerily when everything was neatly attached. 'Let's see what you can do.' He stood back with his arms folded, looking at me as if he were waiting for something.

What do you want me to do?' I said, somewhat confused.

'You tell me. You're the pilot in training.'

This was a different approach, I thought, but am I really in charge? 'Do you want me to just get on with the inflation, then?' I asked hesitantly.

'You're the pilot. Tell me and Paul what you'd like us to do. We'll follow your directions. Don't worry. If you do something really dumb I'll let you know!'

I liked this idea. I felt my new instructor trusted me and I took up the challenge with great interest and enthusiasm. I was very familiar with the procedures now, and having done a successful inflation and take-off on my previous flight, I felt full of confidence.

'OK then. We need to drag out the fabric from the sides before I start the fan,' I told them. 'All three of us can do that.'

This task was easy enough and I was able to start cold inflation almost immediately. As the envelope began to inflate I went inside to unfurl the folds of fabric and flatten the material on the ground. It felt strange to be walking on the soft snow underneath.

'I never go inside like that,' Simon shouted over the noise of the fan as I emerged from the expanding balloon. 'I know other people do, but I hate the sight of mucky footprints all the way up the side of a balloon.'

It hadn't occurred to me before, but it seemed like a valid point. 'Sorry,' I said. 'I'll remember that. Paul, I'll need you to take care of the crown line. Simon, you can hold the mouth open for me.'

It seemed strange giving orders to my new instructor, but I was used to being in charge every day in my job and it soon felt quite natural. I quickly lit the pilot lights and adjusted the position of the burners, directing them to the crown as I had been taught by my previous instructors. This balloon was noticeably smaller than I was used to.

The hot inflation was surprisingly easy and fast. The balloon seemed to rise with very little heat, and once it was in place over the basket strong buoyancy quickly developed, pulling heavily on the quick-release safety strap that Simon insisted on using.

Paul leaned firmly on the side of the basket while my instructor climbed in. It was a snug fit in the smaller basket. With the two of us and three large propane tanks there was very little room for movement, though apparently this basket had been designed to carry three people. I performed all the last-minute safety checks – scoop, lighter, instruments, cables and karabiners – and then we were off.

As we gently cleared the treetops we were greeted by a breathtaking scene. A glorious winter wonderland of snowy fields between clumps of woodland stretched before us as far as the eye could see. Even the bare deciduous trees in their winter mode looked magnificent among the green Canadian pine that protruded so proudly from the deep snow. This is why I'm a balloonist, I thought. Can anything beat the bracing exhilaration of free flight into a scene like this?

'That was a satisfactory inflation and take-off,' Simon told me, interrupting my silent admiration of nature's artwork. I was struck by his noncommittal assessment of my performance, but I knew perfectly well that, with his British background, he would never say something was excellent if it was just good enough.

'Stay fairly low,' he went on as we sailed away. 'About three hundred feet will be fine for now, but I want to see you do some approach-to-landing manoeuvres. We might as well take advantage of all the landing opportunities ahead of us.' He adjusted himself into a comfortable corner and relaxed a little, enjoying the smooth flight in the cold, stable air. 'Just fly along for fifteen minutes or so at this altitude until we reach open country. Isn't this scenery amazing?'

It was amazing, indeed. I found level flying so much easier in the cold temperature and the balloon seemed to need so little heat to stay aloft. I gradually adjusted to the Cameron balloon, and as we leisurely drifted along I felt I was able to converse quite easily while being alert to my surroundings at the same time.

'So what part of England are you from?' Simon asked as we gently drifted over a patch of bare-treed forest.

'I'm a Yorkshireman,' I told him with some pride. ' I'm from Leeds, actually.'

'Ah! Leeds!' he sniffed. 'I thought you must be from somewhere north of the Thames.' We both laughed at this. Even as adopted Canadians, we could still joke about the north-south rivalry that had gone on since time immemorial.

I was suddenly aware that the balloon was falling rapidly. I immediately blasted the double burners in an attempt to break the fall, but as we were flying at such low altitude, I was too late.

We hit the bare treetops in the forest below before the balloon reacted to my input. The basket was inundated with all manner of scrawny branches, which seemed to cover us both from head to foot before we went soaring back into the sky.

This was embarrassment that I didn't need. My first flight with a new instructor and I almost ditch him in the trees. 'Sorry!' I said, red-faced. 'I wasn't watching.'

I looked at Simon as he casually leaned in his corner as if nothing had happened. With infinite calmness and phlegm that only Englishmen seem to have, he pulled off the twigs and pieces of pine that covered him and threw them overboard. 'That was your first test,' he said. 'Your passengers will talk to you all the time. Don't let them distract you from flying the balloon safely. Always be aware of your altitude and the amount of heat in your balloon, especially when you're flying so low.'

My admiration for this man's skills and professional teaching ability was further enhanced by this experience. I tried to imagine what Bill's reaction would have been. It didn't bear thinking about.

The snow-covered fields ahead gave ample opportunity for landing practice. My expert instructor coached me in this difficult manoeuvre. I had to allow the balloon to gradually lose altitude while trying to anticipate the extent of left turn as we approached the ground. At about twenty feet I'd burn again and rise back up to a hundred feet or more.

I did this perhaps a dozen times until I could identify an area ahead and approach it with some accuracy. I felt enormously encouraged by my success and I said as much to Simon. 'I really feel I'm getting the hang of this,' I exclaimed excitedly. 'I almost feel I could really do a proper landing.'

'Not bad,' he replied calmly. 'Not bad at all.' He stood in the corner of the basket, looking ahead like the captain of a ship coming into port. 'Let's go a little higher,' he said. 'Let's see where we are exactly.'

We were still travelling east and as we gained altitude we were able to see further into the distance. The early morning sun was shining now, glittering on the snow and lighting up the surrounding forest and woodland.

I was surprised to see Lake Scugog about a half-mile ahead. I hadn't realized that we had travelled so far – fifteen miles at least – but what a magnificent sight is was. Frozen and snow covered, the lake was a veritable playground for anyone who owned skis, snowshoes or sleds of any kind. It was still early morning, but ice fishermen were already setting up their huts for the day, and several trucks were slowly driving across the thick ice.

Simon was still standing at the front of the basket, peering ahead as we maintained an altitude of 1000 feet. 'OK. I want you to land on Lake Scugog. Pick out your estimated landing spot, do your approach, and land on the ice.'

I was astounded. 'Land on the lake,' I said. 'Will that be OK?'

'Land on the lake. It'll be just fine – and it'll be fun.'

I can't believe I'm doing this, I thought. This is my first unassisted landing and I'm coming down on Lake Scugog. How amazing is that?

I set my sights on a large open area away from the huts and fishermen and coaxed the balloon into a steady descent, burning carefully as required to avoid falling too quickly. I correctly anticipated a slight veer to the left and watched my snowy target come ever closer. A slight breeze was gently blowing over the surface of the lake and I could see wisps of snow billowing up like steam from a kettle.

As we touched down, the basket lightly scraped the snowy surface, rose a few inches, and then made contact with the ice once more. I heard a loud, exuberant cheer from behind, and turning my head, I saw a dozen fishermen dressed in colourful winter gear, clapping and applauding with great excitement and enthusiasm. They came rushing over to greet us as the basket settled in the snow, and we proudly stood there, men from the sky, as they welcomed us and surrounded the basket. To their delight, I occasionally gave a light blast on the burners to keep us inflated. This was exhilaration. This was elation. We shook their hands and chatted, answering their questions, laughing and joking with them. We were celebrities from the heavens and again I relished the moment.

'So what do you think?' I said amidst the noisy exuberance that surrounded us. 'That was my first landing!' I looked at Simon with anxious anticipation.

He smiled, stuck out his hand and said, 'It was good. I enjoyed that.'

As we continued to chat with our welcoming admirers, our chase vehicle appeared on the shoreline and then slowly made its way across the ice to where we waited. Paul parked the truck a few feet away and walked over to join the group, grinning at the attention we had received from the ice fishermen. One of them handed him a snakeskin flask and slapped him on the back. 'Here, have a sip of this stuff,' he said. 'We're welcoming the balloon men!'

It was a leisurely pack up as no one seemed to be in a hurry to leave. The balloon was pulled down and deflated. It seemed to get awfully wet in the process, but with an abundance of help from many willing hands, it was safely packed away and thrown onto the trailer. We stood back and let the fishermen haul the basket and burners to the chase vehicle, allowing them to load the rest of the equipment and lock up the tailgate. The flight was over and we were ready to leave.

Paul drove us away across the frozen lake and soon we were on clear roads, heading for home. It had been a remarkable morning. So much seemed to have happened and still it was only 9.30 on a glorious winter's day. What a wonderful sport – this hot-air balloon thing! I was more determined than ever to pursue it, to involve myself in it, and eventually to share it with passengers of my own.

VII
HIGH ALTITUDES AND COLD DESCENTS

'You're making good progress,' Simon Wills told me one morning after another successful winter flight. He paged through my logbook, checking each item and scrutinizing the scribbled notes he had made along the way. 'You've got more than twelve hours on your logbook now,' he said. 'I can finally see light at the end of the tunnel.'

We were sitting in a small country restaurant, sipping coffee in the company of a couple of tired-looking truckers. It was still only 9 o'clock on a cold March day, but we'd already finished our early morning flight. Sunrise was getting earlier now, allowing us to meet at 5.30 and be in the air an hour or so later. This particular morning had been fairly typical. The flight had been smooth and easy in the cold, stable air and we had done some interesting contouring – flying at treetop level over the rolling countryside. We'd watched a pair of foxes on a rabbit hunt as we scraped along the bare treetops, seen a doe with her two youngsters bounding across the still snowy fields, and finally landed at a friendly farm where we were made most welcome. Paul, our chaser, had been in a hurry to get home and was unable to join us, but now it was very satisfying to have a debriefing session with my instructor over a leisurely coffee.

'We'll have to take a look at what you still need to do to get licensed,' said Simon, closing my logbook with a snap. 'You must have read up on all the details by now.'

'I have, of course,' I replied. 'The twenty hours of burner time is probably the main thing to get finished, but I've been studying for the final written exam as well.'

'That's good,' Simon went on, 'but I was thinking more in terms of the special manoeuvres you'll have to do, like high altitude flights, the cold descent, and tethered balloon regimes – not to mention the solo flights and my requirements for doing some chasing.'

I finished off my coffee as I listened to this long list. 'Tell me about the cold descent,' I said. 'What's that all about?' I was confident about my flying ability and I felt good about being the pilot-under-training (PUT) during my regular instructional flights, but I realized that I still had some distance to go.

Simon leaned back and folded his arms. He obviously liked answering questions like this. 'It's related to your need to learn about emergency procedures,' he stated professorially. 'You are required to do at least one 5000 foot ascent, so I usually combine that with a cold descent. We just simulate a burner break down – turn the pilot lights off and let the balloon fall until you reach about 1000 feet. Then you have to relight the pilot lights, burn like hell, and try to break out of the fall before we hit the ground. Quite fun, really.'

I imagined he had explained it in this manner to other student pilots, hoping to see some fretful reaction at the prospect of falling out of the sky like this. I just looked at him blankly as he sat there with a deadpan expression. I could believe that this manoeuvre would be a little hair-raising, but it was something I desperately wanted to do. 'So when can we do it?' I said calmly. 'I'm ready any time!'

My instructor broke into a smile, knowing that his subtle humour would cut no ice with a fellow Briton. 'Fine,' he said. 'Let's do it next flight – weather permitting, of course.'

Later that afternoon, Simon Wills called me at home. 'I was thinking about that cold descent thing you have to do,' he said. 'You need a fairly calm day to do it and the upper winds, especially, have to be reasonable, otherwise you can get blown forty or fifty miles away in short order. That can be a pain for the chaser. Anyway, the point is the forecast is for calm conditions tomorrow morning and I wondered if you'd like to do it then.'

'Tomorrow morning! I haven't had time to think about it yet.'

'Well, maybe that's the best way. Just get on with it without worrying about it for weeks ahead. What do you say?'

This came as a surprise, but I hesitated only briefly before agreeing. A Sunday morning late winter adventure had its own appeal, but a 5000 foot ascent and cold descent – how could I refuse? Yes, I told him, I'd definitely like to do it.

'That's fine then. I'll meet you at the usual time. By the way,' he added, 'Paul's not available tomorrow, but Laura can chase. She's not done that for a while so she'll be happy to get involved again.'

Laura was Simon's wife. It seems she started out as a student pilot under Simon's instruction, and after a lengthy period of training she obtained her balloon pilot's licence. She was obviously more interested in Simon than in balloons, however. Once she finished training she married her instructor and never flew a balloon again!

The following morning was calm and cool, exactly as forecast by aviation weather. With a temperature of minus five degrees and negligible surface winds, everything was on track for an interesting flight with some unusual peculiarities attached. We met at Simon's house as usual, but this time Laura was in the garage, tinkering with the propane tanks in an attempt to pressurize them ready for the flight. She looked up as I arrived and threw down the enormous wrench she'd been using onto the concrete floor.

'Well!' she exclaimed with her usual cheerfulness, 'I hear things are moving right along with your training. It's all going to happen pretty soon. You'll be the newest balloon pilot in Ontario.'

Laura was always full of life and exuberance, and she could make the most ordinary event thoroughly exciting with her enthusiasm and unqualified gusto. She was ideal for Simon, the cerebral Cambridge graduate, computer whiz and expert balloonist, and he benefited greatly from her lighter approach to life. This morning, of course, we had a thrilling flight plan in place anyway. Laura could hardly contain herself with thoughts of high altitude and cold descent on her mind.

'I remember doing this,' she giggled. 'It was amazing fun, but I was freaking out as we got nearer to the ground. Simon ended up lighting the pilot lights for me, because my hands were shaking so much!'

Simon appeared as we laughed and joked about Laura's experience and my upcoming adventure. 'Morning,' he said stifling a yawn. 'What's the joke?'

'No joke,' I told him. 'We're just reminiscing about previous cold descents.'

'Oh, that,' he yawned, observing the melange of equipment scattered around the floor. He looked over at the nitrogen cylinder, still pulled up against the basket where Laura had left it. 'As you see, we're still pressurizing. It's not strictly necessary at this temperature but it will make a difference.'

The trailer still had to be loaded and Simon, anxious to get moving, started to drag the balloon towards the chase vehicle on the driveway outside. I hurried to help him. 'We'll be using Laura's balloon again – the Pumpkin,' he told me. 'I guess it's got to be the official training balloon now.'

We had used Laura's Pumpkin balloon for almost all my training sessions, especially the more recent ones. It was a 77,000 cubic foot model with a huge, toothy, pumpkin face on it. This size, the so-called Seven, was considered a sports balloon, and it was ideal for training or for carrying up to four passengers on sightseeing flights. I found it far better than the 65,000 cubic foot model we had used on my first few flights with Simon. The basket was roomier and because it carried four fuel tanks rather than three, it had a much greater flying range. I had already decided to buy this model once I had finished training.

With the trailer loaded and ready to go, we headed out on the familiar drive to Mount Albert. Laura drove us with a skill and familiarity that indicated plenty of experience with heavy vehicles and attached trailers, while I sat in the rear seat with my instructor looking at the details of our flight.

'They quoted upper wind readings at 10 knots from 270 degrees for both 3000 and 6000 feet this morning.' Simon was examining his ordnance survey maps as he spoke. 'That's good. Couldn't be much better, really. With winds from the north-west, even at higher altitude, we should be able to land in the Claremont area. I don't want to get too far south.'

Mount Albert was a central location, allowing for flights in any direction, especially on calm days when distances were not much of an issue. High altitude flights were a little different, of course, because wind speeds and directions up there usually bore no relation to what was happening at surface level. This is why an aviation weather report was so crucial. It seemed that Simon had it all worked out and we were in for an interesting experience.

'Have you ever called aviation weather yourself?' Simon settled into a corner, stuffing the sheaf of tattered maps into his flight bag.

'Not yet, no.'

'You'll need to do it, you know. As pilot-under-training you're supposed to get your own report and then make your own flight decisions, based on what they tell you and your interpretation of the details.'

'Maybe I should do that for all future flights, then.'

'I think you should.'

The site at Mount Albert was still covered in snow, though towards the end of winter it was getting a little sloppy and wet. The temperature was creeping above zero on some days now, and we were reaching a time of the year when chasers could be faced with soggy conditions as they attempted to drive into wet fields. It seemed to be no problem this morning, however, and between the three of us we were soon unpacked and ready to inflate.

Simon took the crown line while Laura helped me at the mouth, and a few blasts later the balloon was upright, begging to be released into the beautiful clear sky. Last minute safety checks had become a normal routine for me by now and they were quickly done. Simon clipped down the scoop and hopped into the basket with me. We were ready.

As we slowly ascended from the field, Laura waived us off with a laugh. 'Good luck!' she called. 'Enjoy the sky dive.'

Sky dive, I thought. Is that what we're about to do?

It could have been any normal flight as we gently rose to a flying altitude of about 1000 feet. The breathtaking scene of snow and forest in all directions was still ours to enjoy. We silently approached the occasional small town or village, admired the melting creeks winding their way through the southern Ontario countryside, and we observed the usual wildlife involved in an early morning search for food. I almost wanted to continue the familiar pattern. Maybe we could do a cold descent some other time, I thought, and just enjoy this wonderful peace and tranquillity for now.

My serene reverie was shattered by my instructor's voice. 'Just keep rising at about 200 feet per minute. It'll take us twenty minutes or so, but it's better to rise gently than to go shooting up like a bat out of hell. More fuel efficient too.'

Simon seemed to enjoy these training flights, especially as I could now conduct the whole flight myself. He was taking passenger flights himself in huge eight-passenger balloons several times a week, and it was a pleasant change for him to be flown by another pilot. It gave him time to relax a little and enjoy the beauty of his surroundings. Even with the prospect of a student pilot dropping out of the sky, this remarkable man was as calm and unperturbed as ever. He stood at the short end of the basket, hands stuffed casually in his jacket pockets, looking ahead as I ascended higher and higher into the sky.

'Things look a little different from up here,' Simon observed, looking directly down from his position in the basket. 'It's a while since I was this high.'

We were at 4600 feet according to my altimeter, which I kept strapped to one of the suede-covered uprights. We were still gradually ascending but already we could see over an incredible distance. Lake Ontario lay to the south and we could see a hint of the USA beyond. Lake Simcoe, with its many vacation cottages and beaches, was almost touchable to the north, and the city of Barrie was clearly visible on its western shores. I looked directly down and could see that we were over the Lakeridge ski resort. A few tiny, late-season skiers were slowly drifting down the puny hills in the early morning air. What a sight to behold! Probably staff, I thought, preparing the slopes for a day's skiing.

'Just give it another five or six hundred feet and that should be enough.' I gave a final healthy blast using both burners, and I watched the altimeter's needle gradually shifting towards the 5000 foot mark. We were almost there.

Simon shifted his position, rested his hands on the basket's suede trim edge and looked up into the balloon's huge envelope. He grasped the red deflation line, checking for any tangles, and then gently tested each burner. Satisfied with this, he settled once more against the side of the basket with his hands firmly back in his pockets. The altimeter showed a reading of 5300 feet.

'OK. You can turn the pilot lights off now.' His tone was so ordinary and composed that he might have been asking me to pass him a wrench or a pair of gloves. I thought of Laura in this position. She'd managed to turn the pilot lights off but was unable to relight them because of her shaky hands. I suddenly understood what she meant. I never thought I'd feel this way, but now my heart was thumping and my mouth was dry.

The burners were the life and soul of the balloon. Without them, all control was gone and we were at the mercy of the winds and the weather – and gravity! It would be like losing your brakes on the highway. 'Enjoy the sky dive,' she'd said when we took off. I was about to take that dive now.

Somehow my hands found their way to the pilot light control levers. I swallowed hard and with infinite effort I replied calmly in a voice I didn't recognize, 'No problem. Let's go for it.' Then I firmly and purposefully turned both pilot lights off.

The balloon took on an atmosphere of eerie silence. Without the comforting hum of the pilot lights in the background we seemed to be suspended in space, looking down on a magnificent, silent world of white. For the first two or three minutes nothing happened. The heat in the balloon was sufficient to maintain altitude and we steadily drifted away from the ski resort, heading to the south-east. I looked at the vertical-speed indicator. It showed we were still flying level, but even as I watched, the needle began to move below the zero mark, indicating that the balloon was beginning to fall.

When making an approach for landing a normal rate of fall is about 200 feet per minute, though in some circumstances it can be more. But this was very different. The needle passed the minus five hundred mark then stuck at minus 1000 feet per minute, the limit of the instrument. We were falling at more than 1000 feet per minute, but the instrument could no longer measure our rate of fall!

I looked at Simon as I tried to casually moisten my dry lips. He might have been watching a kids' soccer game as he silently leaned over the edge of the basket watching the earth come ever closer. As we fell, the balloon began to rotate slowly. 'What's happening?' I asked, a hint of panic in my voice. 'Is this quite normal?'

'Quite normal,' Simon replied calmly. 'I'm not sure why it would turn like that, but it seems to do it every time. Probably the scoop catching wind as we fall.' He looked up again into the envelope. 'It's an amazing piece of equipment, though, isn't it? The balloon is like an enormous parachute so we can only fall so fast. If we hit the ground at this speed we'd wreck the basket and break our ankles, but in all likelihood we wouldn't be killed. Amazing!'

This information did very little to console my inner apprehension. We seemed to have been falling for ever. The altimeter showed we were now at 1500 feet. We'd dropped nearly 4000 feet, and the ground seemed to be alarmingly close. Surely we should be burning out of this fall by now. I again put on the calmest voice I could muster up. 'So should I relight the pilot lights now?'

My incredibly cool instructor carefully examined the altimeter with a tight-lipped smile, nodded, and gave a thumbs-up signal. 'Yeah, I guess maybe you could. Go ahead.'

I needed no second bidding. With fumbling hands I opened the propane gas feeders, set the two levers to the ON position, and pressed frantically on the red piezo igniter buttons. Mercifully, the pilot lights reignited immediately, allowing me to fully engage both burners without delay. I blasted them for all I was worth, leaving the barest intermission between each volley. For an eternity nothing seemed to happen, but slowly the balloon stabilized and, to my great relief, the vertical-speed indicator was suddenly reading again. We were falling at 500 feet per minute, then 200, and finally we were at zero, indicating that the balloon was falling no more. The altimeter showed we were at a comfortable 500 feet above ground level. It was over. I'd done it.

'That was unbelievable!' I gasped, slowly regaining my composure. 'That was some experience. But how can you be so cool? What if I'd been unable to relight the burners?'

'Oh, I was ready for any event that might take place,' Simon said from his favourite position on the short side of the basket. 'Those pilot lights can be hard to relight when you're falling so fast. That's why I always keep this thing with me.' He pulled out a butane barbecue lighter from his pocket and effortlessly flicked on the flame. 'If the pilot lights don't work, the flame from this lighter will get the burners blasting, and then the pilot lights will take care of themselves.'

So that was it! As an instructor, Simon maintained a cool exterior disposition, but everything was carefully planned and he was keenly aware of each move his student made. Every possible emergency situation had an exact response. Simon knew what that response was and he was prepared to implement it at a moment's notice. I needn't have worried. I was in safe hands. But I knew that anyway.

We floated along serenely for ten or fifteen minutes. After the tense experience of free fall it was wonderful to relax in the tranquillity of level flight again, observing all the usual sights and sounds of the countryside below us and picking out familiar places and possible landing sites. I could see a small village ahead, surrounded by inviting farms and fields, but at first I couldn't readily identify it.

'No sign of Laura yet,' Simon remarked, looking down at the network of country roads, still quiet with only occasional Sunday morning traffic. Then, looking back, he shielded his eyes with a raised hand. 'Wait a minute,' he said. 'I spoke too soon. I think this is her now. See the truck back there? She's found us.'

The familiar chase vehicle was rattling its way along the gravel road towards the small village ahead. 'That's Raglan she's heading for,' I said, suddenly getting my bearings. 'I recognize the big green barn on the edge of town. We've travelled a lot further than I expected.'

'Try and land at the other side of town,' Simon advised. 'The farm with the big, white silo looks good.'

It was an easy landing in the wet snow with hardly a bounce, but as soon as we touched down Simon called his eager chaser on the radio. 'Don't try to drive in,' he told her. 'You'll only get stuck in the slushy snow. Just bring the two toboggans and we'll slide the stuff out.'

We'd done this a few times before during the winter months. When it was too risky to drive in we'd load the basket and balloon onto toboggans and drag them to the edge of the field. This was hard work, but it was better than the exasperating job of trying to dig out a bogged-down truck.

'You did it, then?' Laura called out across the field as she laboured through the wet snow, dragging the two toboggans behind her. She was a little out of breath by the time she reached us. We had almost finished packing the balloon away and we were ready to start working on the basket and burners.

'Congratulations!' she squealed with her usual high spirits, punching my shoulder much too hard. 'It's always nice to have a new sky diver.' She looked at her husband with a mischievous expression, as if something was supposed to happen. 'Well? Do we initiate him now?'

'No, no! That's for another day,' he mumbled cagily, pushing her aside.

'What's for another day?' I asked, mystified by this conversation.

'Nothing, nothing. Don't worry about it. Don't even think about it.'

They weren't about to tell me anything and I could only imagine what weird and wonderful ritual was planned for me. At least Laura had let the cat part way out of the bag and I could expect something to happen. I didn't know what and I didn't know when, but I didn't care. I'd done my cold descent and I felt great. As Laura said, things were moving right along. There really was light at the end of this tunnel.

VIII
TETHERS, CHASES AND LOST BALLOONS

'You'll probably find tethering as boring as hell. I know I do.' Simon struggled with the enormous jumble of knotted rope that seemed to fill the entire bed of the trailer. I wondered how we had ever managed to fit them in along with the basket, the bulky balloon bag and other assorted pieces of equipment.

'These three tether ropes are each 150 foot long, typical for a normal tether contract,' he explained. 'What you'll have to do first is learn how to attach them securely and safely to suitable anchors and to the balloon itself. We're only going to do this one session on tethering, then at least we can say you've had instruction on how to do it.'

It was about 7 a.m. on a Saturday morning in late March, and Simon, Paul and I were at a small site, a mile or two from Stoneville. The tiny settlement consisted of a dozen houses at the most, but it had the pretentious name of Glasgow. A two-roomed country school, now demolished for lack of students, had once stood on the site, but with its flat, open space it now made an ideal launching spot for balloonists, and we were taking full advantage of its close proximity to Stoneville.

The old baseball diamond, though still a bit wet from the melted snow, provided a solid, level surface, and the surrounding trees gave excellent protection against any surface breeze that might brew up. Simon used the site frequently, either for launching or to check out new balloons by inflating them under tether. But it was also an ideal place for a student pilot to get some tethering experience.

'Shouldn't we have four ropes?' I enquired as we patiently sorted out the pile of well-used hemp rope. 'I thought we'd need one for each corner.'

'It's not necessary. Two ropes hold the balloon from upwind and the third simply prevents it from pulling back from the other side.'

Once the ropes were untangled and stretched out to their full length, we quickly prepared the balloon for inflation in the usual way. Before starting the fan, we attached the ropes to the karabiners on the burner frame using sailors' knots that were designed to be secure and unlikely to loosen or slip. Then it was a question of finding suitable anchors.

Simon picked up one of the ropes at the basket and started to work his way to the other end. 'You can always count on the chase vehicle or trailer for one anchor,' he said. 'If you have two vehicles on site, so much the better. Otherwise you have to look for something else – trees, fences, whatever.'

With the balloon set in the centre of the small field it was a fairly simple matter to anchor down. Apart from the truck, we used the sturdy, wooden fence on the west side of the site and a very convenient tree on the east side that seemed to have been planted there for the very purpose. Paul took care of the inflation under Simon's supervision while I handled the crown line, and the balloon rose quickly to its place of honour, ready to fly away when allowed to do so.

As I clipped the end of the crown line in place, Simon climbed into the basket. He adjusted the scoop and gave a few short blasts of heat to ensure that the envelope was fully inflated. 'OK, Jon, you can replace Paul in the basket now. We can do a few ascents and you can get the feel of a tethered balloon.'

With some awkward shuffling about, Paul and I managed to switch places and I found myself back under the burners as pilot-under-training.

'The important thing is to rise slowly,' my instructor advised as I started to burn. 'Don't underestimate the power of lift. I've seen trucks lifted off the ground before now.'

I wondered if this could possibly be true or whether it was a gross exaggeration. In any case, I could imagine that too much lift would create an awful jolt when the balloon was stopped by the tether ropes, and I took appropriate precautions. I had imagined that the balloon would rise about 150 feet, the length of the ropes, but, of course, that wasn't the case. The height was limited to about 50 feet because the three anchors were set so far away from our lift-off point.

In spite of my precautions, my first attempt at tethered lift ended in an almighty jerk at the end of the ropes.

'Whoa!' Simon exclaimed, but not a bit surprised. 'That nearly threw me clean out of the basket. They'll be suing for damages if you do that at the fairground.'

'The fairground?'

'Of course. The fairground. That's the only reason for learning how to do this. When you have your own balloon they'll always be calling you to do tethered balloon rides at the fairground. It pays well, but it's no good for your balloon, especially with all those kids jumping in and out.'

Over the next half-hour I did about twenty-five tethered ascents, and for most of them I was alone in the basket. I could see what Simon meant, though – it could quickly become very boring. I was sure offering tethered balloon rides at the fairground was something I would never want to do, no matter how well it paid. A balloon is meant to fly free in the open blue sky, not be tied down, squirming and struggling to escape from its earthly tether. As Brian Turner would have said, a balloon is made for blue yonder.

Out of necessity, I quickly mastered the technique of tethered lift, and before too long I could barely notice the bump at the end of the line. Simon quickly lost interest and wandered away, studying his survey maps for the flight to follow, and Paul, equally bored, busied himself with a small repair job on the trailer. When I felt I could bear no more of this up and down monotony, Simon finally strolled back to the balloon and placed his hands on the basket as I descended yet again.

'That's it,' he said, looking quite thankful that it was over. 'Consider yourself trained in tethering techniques. I can put that in your logbook, and it's one more hurdle you've jumped.' He pointed to the fuel gauge on the tanks. 'How much propane have you used?'

'Almost a full tank,' I told him, cleaning the glass face of the gauge with my thumb.

'We'd better take it out, then. You can fill it up on the way.'

He called Paul over to the basket. 'Come on, Paul, it's your turn to fly. Hop in and replace Jon. We'll take off while the balloon is still inflated.' Paul was only too pleased to oblige and again we changed places, struggling to keep out of each other's way.

Simon climbed into the basket and untied the three tethers. He quickly unstrapped the empty tank and lifted it over the edge of the basket for me to put down on the ground. Then, looking at me with a roguish grin that he must have learned from Laura, he chuckled, 'You're the chaser today. Gather up the tethering ropes and load them in the trailer. I'm going to touch down after thirty minutes to pick up the other propane tank. Get it filled up somewhere and have it ready to throw back in the basket. This will be a nice change for you. By the way, the keys are in the truck.'

Everything seemed to happen so quickly at the last minute. A few blasts on the burners and suddenly they were off. As they lifted from the ground it struck me that this was the first time I'd seen the Pumpkin in flight. I'd always been in the basket before. It was an awesome sight, this orange giant with its Pumpkin face smiling down at me, and I could have stood there forever watching its graceful ascent into the sky. But now I had a job to do. I'd better get moving, I thought. I'm the chaser – and I've never done this before.

I hurriedly gathered the tether ropes and threw them into the trailer in a jumbled pile, not having the time to deal with them properly. The aluminium propane tank came next. I knew a service station in Coppin's Corners that could fill it quickly, and I resolved to take care of that task first. I could see the balloon rising slowly and leisurely heading to the north-east and I felt no panic. This should be easy, I thought, as long as I have the Pumpkin in sight, and who could miss this enormous orange giant in the sky?

As I climbed into the truck and prepared to drive away, the radio crackled into life.

'Pumpkin to Explorer.'

'I read you; go ahead.'

'Jon, how's it working out?'

'No problem. I'm on my way now.'

'Good! We're heading north-east but you can expect us to veer more to the east as we gain altitude. I think we'll end up towards Port Perry, but I'll touch down before then – as soon as you have that tank ready.'

I checked my watch. 'I should have it filled in fifteen minutes. I'll contact you then.'

'Sounds good. See you soon. Over and out.'

Everything seemed to be straightforward now, but I knew I'd have to get the fuel tank filled as soon as possible.

I reached the service station in Coppin's Corners within a few minutes, and I was pleased to see the balloon still clearly visible to the south of me, now gently drifting eastward. As I pulled in front of the propane-dispensing unit, a smiling, elderly attendant in badly stained overalls hurried out to greet me. It was still only 8.15 and he seemed delighted to get some business, treating me as if I were the only customer he'd ever had.

'Good morning, sir! What can I do for you?' he smarmed, opening the truck's fuel cap as he spoke.

'No, no!' I told him hurriedly. 'It's not for the truck. I just want you to fill the propane tank. I have the special filler hose and adapter here. I can connect it for you.'

I had been through this procedure several times with both Simon and Bill, and I knew that most service attendants had no idea how to fill the aircraft-rated tanks. We usually patronized the same two or three service stations in the bigger towns, and they were quite used to working with us, but here in Coppin's Corners it was different. This overly polite mechanic was not much help, but between the two of us we managed to get the tank filled in short order.

'I'm in a hurry, you see,' I told him as I thrust some money into his oily hand. I pointed to the balloon, still visible over the distant trees. 'Look, I'm chasing the balloon.'

'Is that balloon yours, then?' he said, shading his narrowed eyes against the early morning sun.

'Well, it's not mine, but I have to contact the pilot before he gets out of range.'

'You mean there's somebody in that thing?' He was absolutely astounded, staring incredulously at the ever-retreating Pumpkin.

'Of course,' I told him. 'The pilot has to fly it. I have to chase it.'

'Well,' he said shaking his head. 'There's some bloody stupid people in this world!'

I jumped into the truck and got on my way, laughing uncontrollably at this curious observation. Is that really the way balloonists were seen by country folk?

I now had to make up some time. Soon I was off the main roads, rattling and bouncing along unpaved country concessions and side roads in a frantic attempt to catch up. After five or six miles, tall trees blocked my view on all sides and although I was aware of the general direction I needed to go, I seemed to have lost sight of the Pumpkin. I called Simon on the radio, telling him I had the full tank of fuel ready, and he replied immediately. The reception was surprisingly crisp, indicating that the balloon was somewhere close by.

'I can see you quite clearly,' he said. 'I'm directly above the truck.'

I pulled over to the muddy shoulder of the country lane and climbed out onto the gravel surface. The distinctive blast of the burners greeted me. Sure enough, the balloon was directly overhead, moving along steadily. No wonder I'd been unable to see it.

'You seem to be moving along,' I called into the microphone. 'Can you see a place to touch down? It looks like nothing but trees here.'

'There's a good, big field half a mile on,' Simon replied. 'There's lots of room and it should be no problem. Don't drive in though. It'll be knee-deep in mud.'

Great! I thought. That's all I need.

I reached the spot in a matter of minutes. It was a huge field with tall trees along the northern side. A wooden fence tracked the whole perimeter, and on the roadside to the south where I had stopped, a deep ditch filled with sloppy, half-melted snow provided an access challenge I didn't need. I couldn't have driven in even if I'd wanted to.

As I slammed the truck door I was just in time to see Simon executing a perfect soft landing towards the centre of the wet field. With a couple of gentle bounces, the Pumpkin settled down in the slushy mud, mocking me with its toothy grin as if it were about to enjoy watching me wade through. A good two hundred yards separated me from the balloon. My task now was to get the full tank of fuel across to the basket. This chasing business was turning out to be hard work.

'OK, we're ready.' Simon's voice floated from the truck's open window. 'There's a bit of a breeze, but I can hold the balloon until you reach us.'

I grabbed the heavy propane tank from the trailer and placed it on the ground. Even though it's made from aluminium, a full tank still weighs almost 80lb and I knew this was going to be a bit of a challenge. Dragging it to the fence seemed to be the best bet. Luckily, the ditch was quite narrow and by straddling it I was able to jump the tank close to the fence and then heave it over the top onto the wet snow at the other side. By the time I'd climbed over the fence myself, I was already worn out and I still had a two hundred yard trek to the waiting balloon.

The Pumpkin smiled incessantly. I fancied it was now laughing at me as I struggled with the fuel tank, first attempting to carry it on my shoulder, then abandoning that idea and dragging it through the slushy snow and mud. Every step soon became arduous and laboured. I silently thanked my lucky stars that at least I was wearing sturdy boots that kept my feet dry in the ankle-deep mud. I struggled to reach the halfway mark, but now I was becoming so physically drained that it seemed impossible for me to make it all the way. But I knew I had to go on. They needed this tank to continue the flight.

Somehow, I summoned up the strength to keep going. I dragged my heavy burden behind me, fighting for breath and praying for the end, but I was now near enough to hear Simon's voice coaxing me along. 'Come on,' he called. 'You can make it.' The Pumpkin swayed and swished in the breeze, laughing at my plight with uncontrolled mirth.

By some miracle, I found myself but three feet from the balloon. I reached out to the basket, unable to go a step further, and Simon, leaning towards me, grasped my hand. He pulled me forward while Paul grabbed the tank and hauled it on board. Leaning against the basket, totally exhausted and fighting for breath, I was quite unable to say a single word.

'Well done! You managed it!' Simon laughed as he smartly strapped the tank in place. 'Take a minute to catch your breath.' He blasted the burners with two or three powerful volleys, and I felt the rapidly developing buoyancy of the balloon as it struggled to be on its way again. The Pumpkin was off once more.

It felt wonderful to be free of the heavy tank. As I stood alone in the middle of the slushy field, I watched the balloon slowly rise and continue its journey. It flashed me one last Pumpkin smile and I managed a silent, belaboured wave before turning to make my way back to the chase vehicle.

The road seemed so far away, but with nothing to drag or carry I made better time than I'd done in my outward trek. The slush and the mud hindered my progress, but within a few minutes I was at the fence once more, calling on my last reserves of energy to climb over and seek the comfort, the incomparable luxury, of the driver's leather seat. With infinite effort, I managed to pour myself over the fence, cross the ditch, and crawl into the truck.

It was sheer heaven to sink back and relax in that seat. I closed my eyes and breathed deeply and steadily, thankful to be off my feet, and immensely satisfied that I had accomplished my mission. I thought of the chasers who had made my balloon experiences possible to this point, and I felt a new admiration and appreciation for them. Chasing is a skill all on its own, I thought. No wonder my instructor believes every pilot should experience it. How else can we appreciate what chasers must deal with every time we fly? It's so easy to take them for granted.

I don't know how long I sat there engrossed in these appreciative musings, but I suddenly woke with a start, wondering momentarily where I was. The balloon, I thought. I'm supposed to be chasing! Where's the balloon?

The Pumpkin was nowhere in sight, but as my view was largely blocked by trees I didn't worry too much about it. I picked up the microphone and tried to make contact with Simon. Nothing! There was not the slightest hint of any reception, only the crackling background noise that told me the balloon was out of range. Not to worry, I thought. Once I'm clear of the trees I should be able to re-establish contact; if I know where they are, I can still be there for the landing.

I started up the truck and continued along the narrow country road. The gravel surface was still partly covered with melting ice and many post-winter potholes of various shapes and sizes. The poor road condition kept my speed to a minimum. After a few minutes I reached a good paved road, which allowed me to drive a little faster, and soon I was able to jog north to the main road into Port Perry. There were few trees here to block my view and I could see several miles ahead towards Lake Scugog and the farms and fields to the south, but still no sign of the balloon.

This is embarrassing, I thought to myself. I'm going to feel like a complete fool if they've landed and I'm not there to retrieve them. I tried radio contact again but as before, the incessant background crackling told me clearly that the Pumpkin was out of range. They've probably given up on me by now, I thought. They'll be stuck in some field wondering where I am.

There was no point in panicking. I knew that. This had to be thought out rationally and logically, so I pulled over to the hard shoulder, stepped down from the truck and did some serious thinking. I looked around me and thought about the possibilities. They had obviously travelled some distance and they were moving in an easterly direction. But Lake Scugog was directly ahead and Simon may have gained altitude in an attempt to drift further south. On the other hand, he may have flown low to travel in a northerly direction before landing. This didn't help much. Should I go north or south?

I decided to drive on into Port Perry. At least I could find a phone there and, if necessary, call Laura to see if she'd heard from Simon. This was a last resort strategy. This is what chasers had to do when they had totally messed up and lost the balloon, and it was something I desperately wanted to avoid.

As I parked on the main street in Port Perry, Saturday morning shoppers were already busy, popping in and out of the many stores and boutiques. I was startled to hear the church clock striking the hour. Ten o' clock! I hadn't realized it was so late. There was no way the balloon could still be in the air now, so there was absolutely no point in searching the skies for its whereabouts. No doubt Simon was packed up somewhere waiting to be rescued. I had no other option but to call Laura.

If this call had to be made, I was thankful that Laura would be the one to answer the phone. At least I was assured that with her sense of humour she would appreciate the funny side.

'Hi, Laura. I'm in Port Perry.'

'Well!' she joked, 'here's the guy who can drop 5000 feet out of the sky but can't keep his eye on an enormous orange Pumpkin!' She'd been expecting my call and she had the directions ready. After some good-natured ribbing and witty remarks, she relieved me of my misery and gave me the information I needed.

'Simon called half an hour ago,' she said. 'He's in Blackstock. Just follow highway 7A to County Road 57. Go south for about three miles and you'll see a farm on the east side. The family name is Baker. They're waiting for you there.'

These directions were clear enough. I thanked Laura and quickly hit the main road once more, glad to be finally on my way. It was closer than I thought. Fifteen minutes later I was at the entrance to a prosperous looking property with a meticulously carved nameplate proudly displayed on a stone pilaster. BAKER, it said simply. I'd found them.

It was a long, winding driveway ending at a large, newly painted farmhouse overlooking several acres of open farmland. My attention was first attracted to the neatly packed-up balloon, basket and burners sitting on a covered porch at the side of the house, all ready to be loaded onto the trailer.

As I turned the corner to the back entrance I was met with an unexpected vision of relaxation and leisure. Simon and Paul were sitting on the full-length wooden veranda with the farmer and his wife, sipping huge mugs of coffee and chatting merrily as if there were no tomorrow. They were deeply settled into comfortable patio chairs with their feet propped up on the low rail surrounding the deck. They looked up as I alighted from the truck, a bit disappointed perhaps that their pleasant interlude was being interrupted. Without moving an inch, Simon greeted me with his usual panache.

'Well, look who's here! If it isn't our chaser!' Then, groaning with the effort, he rose from the chair and introduced me to the Bakers who seemed to be hospitable and friendly folk, very helpful and most interested in the whole procedure of landing and retrieving a hot-air balloon. 'We didn't need the toboggans,' Simon explained. 'Mr. Baker kindly hauled everything out with his tractor. It's all ready to be loaded.'

We wasted no time loading the equipment, and within a few minutes we were saying our thanks and goodbyes to the Bakers. Paul agreed to drive us all back to base and I was finally able to sit back and relax a little, my first attempt at chasing over and done.

'How did you like being the chaser, then?' I noticed an amused tone to Simon's voice and some slight effort to maintain his deadpan facial expression. It's that British thing again, I thought. He knows I've been through hell, and I think some of it was carefully engineered. But I'm not going to fall for it.

'Pretty simple and straightforward, really,' I said calmly. 'I never realized it was so easy.'

IX
SOLO FLIGHTS AND BARBED WIRE FENCES

'I think you're ready to do your first solo,' Simon told me after a debriefing session one morning. 'You know you have to do a minimum of two solo flights before you can get your balloon pilot's licence? Maybe we should think about that soon.'

The thought of doing a solo flight was a bit disconcerting to say the least. Although I had done many successful landings during my winter training, I'd always felt the security of an instructor by my side – someone who could take over if I messed up. Landing a balloon safely is the most difficult thing to learn, and it's during the process of landing that things are most likely to go wrong. On a solo flight it would be all up to me.

We were into early April now and the air wasn't quite as stable as it had been during the colder weather. Early morning breezes were more usual, especially when we were still in the air two or three hours after sunrise. Strong breezes usually meant drag landings – no problem but definitely more challenging! Still, I knew my solo flights had to come sooner or later and I looked forward to them.

My next flight was scheduled for the following Saturday morning and I had convinced myself that a solo was on the cards, but when the day arrived it was obvious that ballooning was out of the question. It was a cold, blustery day. There was no point thinking about it for Saturday, but the aviation weather report seemed to indicate that Sunday morning would be a distinct possibility. As it turned out, the forecast was right. Things settled down overnight, and by Sunday morning conditions seemed to be quite acceptable for some serious ballooning. Early morning surface winds were from the south-west at about 7 knots, allowing us to take off from the Mount Albert site and head towards Sunderland and Cannington.

Simon didn't mention anything about solo flights as we drove up from Stoneville. I wasn't sure about his procedure for this milestone event so I thought it would be better if I said nothing about it either. But I was mentally prepared. If this was to be a solo, I was ready for it, and I was quite excited at the prospect of being alone in the sky.

Once we reached the launch site we followed our normal routines to prepare the balloon for flight. Paul was busy as usual, attending to details about the basket and burners and making karabiner connections from the envelope. He had become very skilled in working around the balloon. He didn't seem to get too many opportunities for flying, but he seemed quite content to plod along, gradually gaining knowledge and skill and realizing that he was still young with plenty of time for training ahead. He took care of the crown line for me with his customary efficiency while I inflated the balloon. Simon casually helped at the mouth and everything seemed perfectly normal.

As I completed the last-minute safety checks, Simon hopped into the basket with me and settled himself into a corner. 'Right,' he said, 'take me on a balloon flight.'

This was a surprise and I felt somewhat let down and disappointed. I'd been quite convinced that I was about to do my first solo, and here was my instructor coming along with me as usual. But it was a beautiful morning. We had an interesting flight ahead of us and I was determined to enjoy it. The solos would come in due course.

As we lifted gently from the ground I thought I saw a subtle signal pass between Simon and Paul, but I paid no attention. Instructors have many messages for students, and no doubt this was simply a reminder to complete all tasks before leaving the site. We continued with our leisurely climb until the now familiar vista of pasture, farms and forest came into view.

The fields were free of snow now and there was a wonderful feeling of spring in the air. Wildlife seemed to be more abundant than ever, and I noticed that cattle occupied some of the distant meadows, and crops were appearing in some of the fields. I'll soon have to deal with new challenges, I thought.

I had reached about 500 feet when I noticed the chase vehicle below us. Paul was staying close as he normally would when we were trying to land, but at this point we'd only been in the air for ten minutes. What was he up to?

'I want you to touch down in this next field ahead.' Simon pointed to a good-sized pasture alongside the main road. 'Just do a normal approach and settle the balloon down in a stand-up landing. The wind is fairly calm so we shouldn't tip. Get as close to the road as you can.'

It began to dawn on me what was happening. The balloon was well positioned for a direct approach to the field, and I quickly slipped into a smooth, gradual descent. I concentrated intensely, feathering the burners as I approached the ground, and I was able to touch down gently as requested.

As the balloon settled into the short grass, my instructor swiftly removed himself from the basket, and holding on to the side with all his weight, he looked at me and gave his final instruction. 'OK, you're on your own. Fly at about 1000 feet for thirty minutes; then contact me on the radio. I won't be contacting you. I'll leave you to concentrate on flying this balloon. Good luck!'

With that, Simon released me on my first solo balloon flight. Without his weight the Pumpkin rose rapidly into the sky, even before I had a chance to apply heat from the burners, and I found myself at 300 feet and on my journey, long before the balloon had a chance to stabilize. I glanced down and saw Simon, now out of the field, leaning on the chase vehicle with arms folded in his typical cool fashion. He watched me for a minute more, then climbed into the truck with Paul. The chase was on.

I slowly grasped the immensity of what was happening. Here was I, alone in the sky, with no one but myself to get me down. It was exhilarating and slightly fearful, but I couldn't compare it to any other feeling or experience I'd ever had. I could feel my heart pounding, much as it had done during my cold descent, but this time there was no instructor at the ready with emergency plans of action. Only my own plans counted now.

At 1000 feet I levelled off and tried to maintain a steady altitude and direction. I could see Lake Scugog to the right of my flight path and Lake Simcoe to the left. I knew I would travel between them and that was good. Many open fields and opportunities for landing were ahead of me and that gave me confidence. It would be just a normal landing like the ones I had done so many times before. The fact of being alone, I told myself, was purely incidental.

As the time passed my confidence and relaxation increased. With only my weight, the balloon responded to the slightest input of heat, and I found I was able to fly with great precision and accuracy. By the time my thirty minutes had passed I was already experiencing a thrilling feeling of accomplishment, and I contacted the truck with the firm, confident voice of an experienced pilot.

'Pumpkin to Ford!'

'Come in. I'm receiving you.'

'Simon, I've done thirty minutes. What's next?'

'We have you in sight. Start looking for a landing spot. We'll stay with you.'

'Directions understood. Over and out.'

I could see several landing opportunities a few miles ahead. Some fields had been ploughed and prepared for planting, but thankfully, I could see no cows. At least, I thought, that's one problem I won't have to contend with.

I allowed the balloon to begin a steady descent and I prepared myself mentally and emotionally for the most difficult phase of my first solo flight. As I lost altitude I veered typically towards the left. A wooded area now lay in my flight path. No problem, I told myself, open fields are visible a mile or so beyond the woods; I'll fly at treetop level until I reach them. I'd done this many times before and it was always a most enjoyable experience, usually offering a chance to see a variety of wildlife in the woods. My flight was almost over.

I skimmed the tops of the trees as I crossed the woods, catching a glimpse of a handsome, big-horned buck as he drank from the babbling creek. I had become used to the lower weight in the basket now. It was a pleasure to fly with such precision and I felt utterly confident in my ability to maintain level flying over the trees.

I noticed a tall, dead tree fifty yards ahead of me and to the left of my flight path. It protruded twenty feet above its neighbours, and its tangled mass of dead branches seemed to stretch out in all directions like grasping, spiny hands. I was thankful that I was well clear – or so I thought! Bill Bauer had once told us, only half jokingly, that if a balloon pilot attempts to land in a large meadow containing only one tree, the balloon will inevitably head directly for that tree – that's Murphy's law! Now, to my horror, I saw this law being applied at treetop level.

For no apparent reason, the Pumpkin aimed itself at the only obstacle for miles around. I was suddenly flying directly at the dead tree, its malicious, sharp limbs eagerly waiting to tear the balloon to bits. I instinctively burned fiercely and furiously in an attempt to escape. The balloon began to rise within a few feet of this coniferous ogre, and fortune seemed to be on my side. To my great relief, rather than hit the tree directly, the Pumpkin merely brushed its side as I speedily took to the skies.

This narrow escape inflicted a significant dent in my self-confidence. If I'd hit that tree head on, I thought, I would at this moment be stuck in the middle of the woods with a severely ripped-up balloon. It didn't bear thinking about.

The sudden, intense input of heat had caused me to gain some unwanted altitude, but now I was steadily falling again. I was well clear of the woods and I could see several fenced pastures ahead. They were all clear of animals but from the air, they seemed rather small. Nevertheless, after my close brush with disaster I was determined to land as soon as possible, and I allowed the balloon to continue its steady descent.

A small farm lay ahead and I realized that the path of my descent was taking me directly to the centre of a paddock at the side of the barn. It's small, I thought, but that's where I'm landing.

Some steady feathering of the burners allowed me to touch down at my intended spot, but the contact with mother earth was somewhat harder than usual, causing an enormous bounce towards the barbed-wire fence ahead. I had no choice but to rip out the top and deflate. The basket tipped and I watched the Pumpkin unceremoniously drape itself over the barbed wire, some miscellaneous farm implements, and all the muck of the barnyard. I was down. I'd done my first solo.

This was supposed to be a moment to celebrate, but after my dismal landing I was in no mood for celebration. I'd done so many perfect landings before with an instructor at my side. Why did my first solo have to end like this? I could have kicked myself.

As I crawled out of the tipped basket I saw the chase vehicle in the laneway by the modest, white farmhouse, where Simon was talking animatedly to the property owner. I was struck by the way the farmer seemed to be enjoying the joke, laughing and pointing in my direction. At least we seemed to be welcome. I walked to the fence to see if I could fathom some way of removing the envelope from the barbed wire. Paul wandered over and joined me there.

'Nice landing!' He said with a grin. 'We watched you come down.'

'Nice landing, eh? What does Simon think?'

'Oh, you know Simon. He's seen it all before and much worse. He's sure to rib you about it, though.'

'That's what I'm afraid of.'

We started to fold back the fabric of the envelope in an attempt to gather the material into a manageable roll when Simon interrupted us.

'Don't do that!' he called as he walked over to join us. 'There's a technique to this. We want to avoid any more tears on the fabric.' He disconnected the karabiners on the burner frame and wound up the flying wires into their usual neat coils. 'We have to stuff the envelope into its bag bit by bit, dragging it along until we reach the fence. Then we can simply tumble the bag over and no harm will be done.'

It seemed to be a simple matter, and it worked well. I was relieved that Simon didn't see it as a big deal. So far he had said nothing about my solo and we packed up as usual as if it were any normal training flight. We dragged the balloon over to the chase vehicle, and as we finished loading it into the trailer, Simon looked at me quizzically, as if he had been expecting some kind of explanation. 'So what's the story behind the big rip then?' he asked, noisily closing the tailgate and locking it into place.

I was momentarily stunned. 'What big rip?' I asked, genuinely puzzled at the question.

'The big rip in the balloon. How did it happen?'

'I'm not aware of any rip in the balloon.'

'But didn't you notice it just now as we packed it away.'

'No, I'm afraid I didn't. Did it catch on the barbed wire?'

Simon shook his head and leaned on the truck. 'We watched you land and the rip was obvious as you came in. It's no big deal. It's in the lower third and it won't affect the balloon's flying ability, but something must have happened on your flight.'

I suddenly realized what had happened. That wretched tree with its scrawny, grasping branches must have ripped a piece out of the Pumpkin as I brushed by. I told Simon what had happened and he managed a sympathetic grin. 'We all rip balloons,' he said, 'but you can tell Laura yourself. We had the Pumpkin specially made for her. It's her balloon.'

Now I felt really bad. I knew it would be fast and inexpensive to get the balloon repaired, but it was a depressing end to the morning. My first solo, which had started out so well, had ended with a damaged balloon and a messed-up landing. What a way to go!

The three of us climbed into the truck, ready to move on, but Simon sat there in the driver's seat, apparently in no hurry to drive away. After a minute or two of pondering and occasionally glancing at the sky, he turned to face me.

'You're probably feeling pretty bad now, eh?'

'You could say that.'

'Right, well I think there's only one solution.'

'What's that, then?'

'I think you should do another solo right now.'

It took a moment for this idea to sink in. 'Another solo?' I said, sitting up straight on the narrow back seat. 'You mean I should do another flight right now, from this farm?'

'Not from here, no. I think we should drive down to Glasgow. It's still only 8.45 and the wind is light from the south-west. Even if the winds pick up a bit it should be a good flight. If you don't do it now you'll only fret about it all week, and that won't do your self-confidence any good.'

This seemed to make good sense and I agreed immediately. If I could do a perfect solo now, my first attempt wouldn't matter so much, and Simon was right, I wouldn't have to go through the whole week worrying about it.

Simon drove us down to the site at Glasgow using a network of country roads that had become very familiar to me over the past few months. We made good time in the peaceful ambiance of an early Sunday morning and the three of us were soon busily engaged in our second inflation of the day. The surface winds had picked up slightly, causing the balloon to roll about as the fan pumped cold air into the envelope, and the unsightly ripped panel was now all too evident, flapping in the breeze as we worked around the balloon.

As the balloon came up both Simon and Paul needed their full weight to keep the basket firmly on the ground. The Pumpkin rolled and swayed in the breeze, anxious to be in the air once more, and I could see that this was going to be a windy take off, calling for more attention and concentration than usual.

'This will be good experience for you, taking off in windy conditions,' Simon told me as I checked the karabiners and flying wires. 'You'll probably have a drag landing, but you've done it all before. Rip out if you have to. Fly for thirty minutes at 1000 feet or so and then land. We'll stay with you. Good luck, again!'

They released their hold on the basket and once more I was in the air on a solo flight. The conditions were considerably different to those of my earlier flight. I was moving much faster now and I would obviously travel much further. I levelled off into a smooth and steady flight path at 1000 feet. Before long I could see the town of Uxbridge ahead and the many open fields and meadows beyond. I felt competent again as I felt the most subtle responses to my burner blasts. I was determined that this would be the perfect solo.

As always, it was a magnificent view and I was soon caught up in the incomparable exhilaration of being in the air. Lake Scugog shimmered in the distance, now bathed in sunlight as the morning progressed, and it seemed like an eternity since my first flight of the day when I had observed it then. Occasionally, I looked down on the network of roads below. Simon and Paul were with me all the way and I felt secure in the knowledge that they would be there for my landing.

A half hour of flying time seemed to pass very quickly. I would have been happy to continue, but I knew that for solo flights a duration of thirty minutes was the minimum requirement of the Ministry, and all we needed to do this morning was fulfil that requirement. I decided not to contact Simon by radio this time. Instead, I set my mind on selecting a good landing spot and manoeuvring into a steady, stable descent.

Several open fields lay ahead of me and I could have selected any one of them. I decided on the second one along because of its close proximity to the road and easy access for the truck. I caught sight of the chase vehicle as I gradually lost altitude. My instructor was still with me. Good, I thought, this time he can see a good landing.

My approach, though stable and controlled, was considerably faster than average and I anticipated a tip landing and a short drag across the field. My prediction was accurate. I hit the ground at almost the exact spot I had selected. The basket fell gracefully to its side, and slid along the wet grass as I vigorously pulled out the deflation line to its full extent. The smiling Pumpkin collapsed and, as the basket came to a smooth stop, it settled into the grass and lay peacefully on the ground, fully deflated. I was down again. But this time I had executed the perfect drag landing.

Simon was in the field even before the basket came to a stop, running alongside while Paul drove through the open gateway. 'Great landing!' he laughed as I crawled out of the basket for the second time that day. 'Your whole flight from beginning to end was excellent. The conditions were more difficult, but you handled everything perfectly. Congratulations!' He shook my hand enthusiastically, and Paul, now stepping down from the truck, did the same. 'Now we can really celebrate,' he said.

This is what I needed to hear. There would have been no point in celebrating an unsuccessful solo, but now all the stops were pulled out and I sensed an excitement that I thought must surround every first solo.

Simon was in a much more relaxed and jovial mood now and he chatted enthusiastically as we packed up and loaded the equipment once more. 'It's always an exciting milestone when someone does his first solo,' he exclaimed. 'As an instructor, I get a great thrill out of it. Sorry I was so blah about your first attempt, but if you rip the balloon and drape it over a barbed-wire fence you can hardly get excited about it.'

'Too true,' I agreed.

Paul produced an impressive bottle of champagne from a box in the trailer after receiving a subtle signal from Simon. He brought it round to the side of the truck and the three of us laughed and joked as we fiddled with the wire cap that held the cork securely in place.

'Now this has to be done right,' Simon chuckled, taking the bottle from us and carefully loosening the cork. You have to keep this cork for the rest of your life as a souvenir of your first solo. Now, Jon, kneel down.'

'Kneel down?' I asked suspiciously.

'Kneel down; that's what I said.'

I was feeling so euphoric at that moment that I would have stood on my head if asked to do so. I'd expected some kind of initiation so I knelt down on the grass at once, ready for anything that might occur. Simon had the cork almost ready to pop when he proclaimed the balloonist's welcome, 'You have left the earth and flown to touch the sky. You have flown with the eagle and the hawk. And you have returned safely to Mother Earth. By this sign, Mother Earth welcomes you back into her arms.' He then planted an enormous handful of black earth firmly on my head, followed by half a bottle of expensive champagne! It was pure elation! The three of us laughed hysterically as I attempted to clean myself up, and we socialized merrily for some time after before finally finding some plastic glasses and finishing off the bottle of champagne. This was truly a milestone in my training and I realized that I had completed the last mandatory licensing requirement by doing two solos instead of one. My instructor had been so right in pushing for the second solo that morning. Now I could go home with a feeling of accomplishment instead of a depressing feeling of disappointment.

The hilarity continued throughout the drive back to Stoneville. I was an absolute mess, covered in mud, sweat and champagne, but I couldn't have felt better. Simon, still upbeat and probably feeling good that my training was essentially finished, happily confirmed my present status. 'You've fulfilled all field requirements now,' he said. 'Only the final exam to do; then you can officially join the ranks of fully qualified balloon pilots.'

'That's a great thought,' I returned, 'but before that, I have one other obligation.'

'What's that, then?'

'I have to explain to Laura how I put such an enormous rip in her beloved Pumpkin!'

X
EXAMS, LICENCES AND MIXED-UP QUALIFICATIONS

With the completion of two solos, my field training was technically finished, and all I had to do now was pass the final written exam. But Simon was never satisfied with bare minimums. He called me during the week, suggesting that one more supervised solo would be in order, and in any case, he said, we would need to get together before the exam to review all the paperwork and make sure all requirements were properly documented.

'I have to give you a letter certifying that you've completed everything satisfactorily,' he explained. 'If you could do a solo flight one evening this week we could follow it with one last debriefing session and go over everything, including the subject matter for the exam.'

This seemed to be a good idea. I had studied a mountain of reference materials and various publications on the technical aspects of free-flying balloons, but I had several queries and a final chance to discuss some of them with Simon would be appreciated. Besides, I still didn't have a balloon of my own, so getting one more flight in the Pumpkin would be an added bonus.

I watched the weather carefully during the week, but good flying conditions didn't materialize until Friday, which was a relatively calm day. Sunset was getting noticeably later towards the end of April. This made evening flights more feasible and it allowed plenty of time to get myself ready after school and head up to Stoneville.

Simon was ready and waiting when I arrived at his house. 'We've got no chaser this evening,' he told me, dragging an unfamiliar balloon towards the trailer. 'Paul couldn't make it and Laura's working, so it's just the two of us.'

I looked curiously at the smaller canvas bag. 'What's this, then?' I asked.

We're using the 65 for this flight,' he told me, giving a tight-lipped smile. 'The Pumpkin's out for repair – remember?'

'I do, indeed! How much is that going to cost?'

'Not much. I'll send you the bill when I know.'

In many ways I preferred evening flights. The surface winds inevitably became calmer in the evening as the sun sank lower in the sky, and this usually guaranteed a soft and gentle landing. Morning flights tended to be the opposite. There was always some degree of anxiety in trying to land before the mid-morning winds whipped up.

With the gentle weather conditions, the two of us were able to inflate the balloon with no problem, and the calm and steady south-west breeze allowed for an easy take-off at the Glasgow site. I followed a flight path that was similar to the previous week's solo, but with different flying conditions I knew that I would cover a shorter distance. I thought I might make up for that by flying longer.

I was disappointed at not being able to fly the Pumpkin, of course, but I had only myself to blame for that. But this was a chance to fly a different balloon and I could only benefit from experimenting with its different flying characteristics. It was an enjoyable hour, and I touched down before reaching Uxbridge, short of the open fields where we had celebrated my first solo landings the previous week.

'It's getting to be old hat already,' Simon announced, laughing heartily as he drove up to where I stood in the empty pasture. 'That was another great solo for your logbook. We should head back quickly now and get all this paperwork finalized.'

It was hardly old hat to me. Every flight was a thrill, and though I felt my skills solidifying and my knowledge of the balloon increasing with every flight, I still thoroughly enjoyed every moment of it. I looked forward more than ever to having my own balloon.

It was a great feeling of satisfaction as I sat at Simon's kitchen table that evening, talking as a student pilot for the last time. He pulled out a file folder and opened it to reveal a sheaf of notes and papers, some of which were headed by official-looking government logos.

'Well, you've done everything now,' he said, picking up the sheaf. He placed the papers back in the file one by one as he reamed them off. 'High altitude, cold descent, tethering, chasing, twenty-one hours burner time, full flight routine, landings, three supervised solos, ground school. . .'

'Ground school?' I queried, interrupting his careful review. 'I haven't done a ground school for balloons.'

'Of course you have. The ministry requires a ten-hour ground school in such things as meteorology, air regulations, navigation and so on, but that doesn't mean it has to be in a classroom situation. When it's only one student I always do it on a one-to-one basis at the launch site, or as we are doing right now in a debriefing session. This is your ground school at the kitchen table.'

'Oh, I see! Yes, I suppose I have covered everything that way over the past few months. So I guess it's just the final exam now.'

Simon ran his finger down the list of licensing requirements again. 'You know there are two exams, don't you? Did you already write Air Regulations?'

'I did that last October,' I told him. 'I'd already done one for ultralight planes, but I was told I'd have to do it again for balloons. It was a breeze, really. I got over 90%.'

'That's fine, then. So it's just the balloon pilot's exam. Let's look at the topics.'

The list of required topics was quite formidable, covering a diverse area of knowledge from balloon construction, stress limits and instrumentation to the wider area of knowledge required of balloon pilots, like weather patterns, aviation charts and the medical implications of flying at high altitude. I'd felt well prepared before, but I found my final discussion with Simon extremely useful, and by the time we'd finished I was confident I could do better than the required 75% pass mark.

Simon planted his coffee cup firmly on the table. 'So, when are you going to write the exam,' he asked, leaning back in his chair.

'Next week sometime, all being well.'

'Good, it's best to just get it out of the way.'

'I'll have to go down to the DOT Region Office in Toronto again. It's like a maze in that place with all the different departments. I can never find my way around.'

Simon laughed, knowing full well what I meant. He reached for a glossy brochure on the nearby shelf. 'Once you've done the exam we should order your balloon from England,' he said. 'It can take about a month to get here, so if you want to do some ballooning when you get your licence we should move on it soon.'

'Yes, I was wondering about that. I'll have to get some money put together. Then we can look at the options.'

I left Simon's house with a sense of accomplishment. As I drove home I thought of the long process I'd been through since my flight over the Yorkshire Dales with Brian Turner the previous summer. I recalled the flights with Bill in the fall, the winter flights, landing on frozen Lake Scugog and my recent solos. I was on the verge of being a fully qualified balloon pilot now. I was ready for the exam and I'd be taking this final step in a matter of days. I was almost there!

~

'I have to go out for a while today,' I told my secretary as I arrived at school the following Friday morning. 'I have an exam to write.'

'An exam? My goodness, I thought you'd finished with exams long ago.' Terri followed me into my office with a pile of papers for my attention and placed them on my desk. 'What kind of exam is it? Another of those ministry refresher programmes?'

'Yes, it is a ministry exam, actually. Ministry of Transport balloon pilot's exam.'

'Oh, that,' she said nonchalantly. She had heard all about my progress towards being a balloon pilot over the previous few months, and though she had found it quite fascinating at first, she had long since lost interest. 'You'll be able to give us all a balloon ride when you're done.'

I smiled to myself. I enjoyed my double life. I could sit there in my suit and tie, the academic administrator, leading educator and ultimate authority of the school, but on weekends I was someone different. Then, dressed for the rough and tumble of the countryside, I was an aviator, and soon with my new balloon I'd be sharing the thrill of gentle flight with passengers of my own. But first I had an exam to pass!

I arrived at the transport region offices just before noon. Although I had been twice before, I still found it necessary to ask for directions at the information desk.

'All aviation matters are dealt with on the sixth floor,' sniffed the important-looking security guard behind the counter. 'You'll find the elevators past the food court to your left.' He pointed the way with no hint of a smile.

As I emerged from the elevator at the sixth level I recognized the large waiting area from my previous visits. It was bordered by leather-padded counters, each staffed by bustling, well-dressed women going about their business. Several doors with opaque glass windows led off into various rooms, some of them marked as examination rooms with impressive lettered signs. Nervous pilots sat on the comfortable leather seats all around the room holding number cards and waiting for attention. Pilots always seem to have this same look about them, I thought – short hair cuts, neatly trimmed moustaches, and inevitably wearing short-sleeved, blue shirts.

I took a number and joined the group, choosing a seat next to a bespectacled young man in his early thirties. He smiled and nodded as I sat down. 'Are you writing an exam?' he asked nervously, an obvious candidate himself.

'Yes,' I told him, 'balloon pilot's exam.'

'That's interesting,' he replied. 'I'm here to do the fixed wing written paper for commercial airlines. I've been training for months and if I can pass the exam today I have a new job waiting for me. I have to pass, but I never thought I'd be so nervous.'

I smiled sympathetically. 'If you've studied you'll be fine,' I told him. 'Good luck.'

His number was called soon after and I watched as the young woman behind the desk thoroughly scrutinized his sheaf of application papers and then handed him a large envelope and pointed him to Examination Room 3. He thanked her profusely, walked awkwardly across the floor and disappeared behind the door like a lamb to the slaughter.

My turn came a few minutes later. I handed the same young woman my completed application form along with Simon's documentation, my logbook, my medical information and my cheque for the examination and licence fees. She was wearing an official identity tag on the lapel of her business suit, showing that her name was Amy.

I was impressed with the scrutiny she applied to every detail. Finally, she drew a large brown envelope from the filing cabinet behind her and handed it to me as if it contained the deeds to Buckingham Palace. This is your examination paper,' she said carefully and distinctly. 'Take it to Examination Room 2 and check in with the invigilator. You'll be allowed two hours. When you've finished, bring the completed test back to me.'

I thanked her and walked confidently over to Room 2, entering as quietly as possible. A dozen or so candidates sat at individual desks, labouring over various aviation exams, some using calculators and slide rules, others making side notes or completing final versions of their answers on impressive government answer sheets.

An austere invigilator in his sixties sat at a large, important-looking desk facing the exam candidates. He raised a finger to his lips as he saw me enter, indicating that I mustn't disturb anyone in the room. I smiled and nodded, and he took the envelope from me, making a note of the large reference number clearly displayed on the top corner. After checking the time on the wall clock above his head, he handed back the exam envelope and pointed to an empty desk at the front of the room. With an exaggerated whisper he told me what I already knew. 'You'll be allowed two hours,' he whispered. 'It's 12.15 now; you'll have to finish at 2.15.'

I thanked him in a whisper meant to rival his own and sat down at the assigned desk. I opened the envelope and removed its contents, inadvertently rustling the papers as I did so. This caused the invigilator to look at me sternly. I tried to be more careful. Soon I was well organized and I set to work on the exam, determined to score the highest mark I possibly could.

I began by glancing through all the questions quite quickly, making mental notes about easy questions and those that seemed more difficult. There seemed to be a large number of obscure questions, but I was not overly worried. I knew they'd become clearer when I spent some time on them, and I had plenty of time.

Over the following hour or so I answered questions on meteorology, navigation, aviation maps and charts, and medical conditions as they relate to flying. I was ready for difficult physics questions on stress distribution, load-to-volume ratios and temperature versus lift capability, but I searched in vain for any questions in these areas.

Some questions I felt were quite unfair, requiring sophisticated calculations of aircraft wing areas, which had to be used to judge an aeroplane's ability to fly at certain speeds. Fortunately, I had taught high school maths and sciences for a number of years, and I was able to muddle through, but I found it annoying that the ministry would expect balloon pilots to understand all the intricate details of fixed wing aircraft. Some questions I simply couldn't answer at all as the material was outside my range of aviation study topics.

Eventually, I finished answering all the questions I could manage. It was only 2 p.m. and I still had fifteen minutes to go, but as I'd reviewed my answers several times, I felt there was no point staying in the examination room any longer. I gathered up my papers and prepared to leave. My chair scraped the floor as I stood up, making a dreadful noise, and I thought the invigilator would burst a blood vessel as he looked up, startled, his face flushed with annoyance. His eyes followed me to the door and I slipped out as quietly as I could, thankful to be away from this strict supervisor who took his job so seriously.

Amy was still bustling behind the counter in the waiting area. There were only two pilots waiting for attention now and things were not quite so hectic. When she saw me approaching she came over immediately and smiled pleasantly. 'How was it?' she asked, taking the papers from me and stacking them into a neat pile.

'A bit different to what I was expecting,' I replied. 'I'm not even sure I've passed.'

'Oh, well,' she went on, showing some semblance of sympathy. 'We'll see when it's been marked and graded. I'm sure you've done very well.'

Amy was obviously more confident than I was.

'How long will it take before I get the results?' I asked. 'Is it the same as for the Air Regulations exam?'

'Oh, yes. Of course. The markers are right here every day. They'll have it done in half an hour. Go and have a coffee and be back here just after 2.30. It'll be ready for you then.'

I was hoping she'd say that. At least I wouldn't have to worry about it, waiting for the results. I'd know right away whether I'd passed or failed.

It was a long coffee break. The time seemed to drag as I wandered back and forth, paper cup in hand, and I became more and more anxious about my results. With such a high pass mark there was every chance that I'd failed. I was still annoyed at some of the questions and I wanted to complain that the study guide was out of date, but then I wondered if perhaps Simon had not kept up with recent changes and he'd given me some outdated materials. I'd certainly let him know next time I spoke to him.

I returned to the examination area thirty minutes later as requested, and Amy greeted me once more, pulling out my file from a slot under the counter. 'I have everything here for you,' she smiled, shuffling through my application forms and supporting documents. 'Now, your exam results.' She produced a government document that she must have received from the markers and placed her stylish glasses on the end of her nose. 'The pass mark for this exam is 75%. Now your score is. . .' She ran her finger down the list of figures on the sheet while I sweated with anticipation. 'Your score is 75%. That's cutting it pretty fine, but it means you've passed. Congratulations!'

I sighed with relief, but I wasn't used to passing tests by the skin of my teeth, and although I knew that this young woman wasn't to blame, I couldn't resist making some comment about the exam content.

'Thanks,' I said, 'but I'm quite disappointed as I was aiming for 100%. I really can't understand why balloon pilots need to be tested on fixed wing dynamics. Many of those questions didn't reflect the syllabus guidelines, and they were quite irrelevant to the flying characteristics of a hot-air balloon.'

Amy looked at me in stunned silence. Then, with shaking hands, she fumbled with the pile of papers before her and extracted my licence application form and the sheet showing my exam results. After examining them for a few seconds she clapped her hand to her mouth and stared at me with wide-open eyes. 'My God!' she said hoarsely. 'I gave you the wrong exam!'

It was my turn to be stunned. 'The wrong exam? What on earth do you mean?'

'I gave you the exam for commercial airline pilots! For fixed-wing aeroplanes!'

I didn't know whether to laugh or cry. I just stood there, speechless. We stared at each other, waiting for the other to speak until I heard myself saying, 'So what am I supposed to do now?'

Amy looked at the large clock on the wall and then at her dainty wristwatch. 'I suppose you'll have to write the balloon pilot's exam. You still have time; it's only 2.45 and you're allowed two hours. This office closes at 5 o'clock.'

'But I've just spent two hours writing an exam! I'm supposed to spend another two hours in that room?'

'You can always come back another day if you wish. It's up to you.'

I pondered this for a minute, then looking at her squarely I said, 'I'll do it now. There's no way I'm coming back. I want to finish all my licence requirements today. That's what I planned and that's what I'll do.'

Amy nervously rooted in the cabinet and took out another brown envelope. She examined the code very carefully before she handed it to me. 'I'm so sorry for the mix-up,' she said. 'I don't know how I could have been so stupid.'

'Well, mistakes do happen,' I replied stoically. 'It can't be helped now. I'll just have to write the proper exam, won't I? I suppose it's Room 2 again?'

'It is, I'm afraid, yes.'

I turned and headed once more for the examination room, this time a little less enthusiastically than before. 'Look at the bright side,' Amy called softly. 'You're qualified for fixed wing now!' I looked over my shoulder as I reached the door and we both laughed at the absurdity of the whole thing.

The invigilator was astonished to see me coming back. He looked at the lone pilot who was still writing and then at the clock as if he had been hoping to leave soon. I had obviously ruined his plans. 'Which licence exactly are you trying to get?' he whispered impatiently, taking the envelope from me and noting the code on his list.

'I've finished fixed wing,' I said sarcastically, 'so I thought I might as well do balloon pilot while I'm here!'

He frowned heavily and hurriedly handed back the exam. 'Two hours,' he told me gruffly. 'Sit anywhere you want,' and he sank back into his chair with a deep sigh.

This is more like it, I thought, quickly glancing through the questions in the examination booklet. The questions on meteorology and navigation were very similar to the ones I'd just dealt with on the fixed wing exam and I was able to complete them in short order. I was well prepared for the rest too. Load tape stresses, acceptable repairs, interior temperature awareness and other specific balloon questions were clear and straightforward. I eagerly set down my answers, feeling very confident now but greatly looking forward to the end of this ordeal.

By the time I had finished, an hour and a half later, I was alone in the room with my unhappy friend. It was only 4.20 and he seemed relieved that I had finished early. As I prepared to leave I saw him quickly packing up his briefcase and gathering his belongings. He followed me out of the door in a great hurry as if he had to catch the last bus home.

Amy was still behind the counter. The place was deserted now and she was leaning against the back ledge with her arms folded, looking a little bored. She smiled as I came over to the counter and took the finished exam from me. 'You're early,' she said. 'How was it this time?'

'Much better,' I told her. 'I'm just glad it's over.'

She looked at the clock and again compared the reading with the time on her wristwatch. 'I'll see if I can get one of them to mark it right away. They won't do it after 4.30, you know, but I think we'll just about manage it.' She disappeared through a door marked "Private", and left me waiting and wondering.

'It's fine,' she announced cheerfully as she emerged a few minutes later. 'It shouldn't take long. Your exam is the last of the day and they've got nothing else to do.'

After about fifteen minutes, a gentleman with a short haircut and moustache appeared at the counter. He whispered something to Amy and gave her an official-looking document, throwing a cursory glance in my direction before hurrying back to the mysterious, secret world of exam markers.

Amy smiled widely as she examined the sheet. 'Wow! You did well,' she said, as I approached the counter once more. 'You've got 97% for this one!'

It wasn't unexpected. I knew I'd done well. 'That's the difference when you do the right exam,' I told her, finally feeling that this day was nearly over.

Amy gathered up my application and supporting documents, including the most recent one showing my exam score. 'Everything's here now,' she said, looking quite relieved that things had turned out right in the end. 'I can put this in for processing. It'll take a while, but you should receive your balloon pilot's licence in the mail within ten days, anyway. Congratulations!'

It was a long drive home in the Friday evening rush hour. As the traffic slowed down on the highway I noticed a car bumper sticker in front of me. "I'd rather be flying" it said in bold blue letters. Yes, I thought, so would I.

I slowly absorbed the reality of my current pilot status. I'd now done everything I had to do. I'd finished my training and I'd passed my exams. All I needed now was the piece of paper that says so.

Amy must have fast-tracked my application because my licence arrived in only four business days. Naomi came in with the mail the following Thursday evening and looked at me with a knowing smile. 'Something for you, I believe,' she said, handing me an envelope decorated with the familiar government logo.

It was the culmination of a challenging eight months of study and training, and it was with pride and satisfaction that I scrutinized every detail of my new licence. I looked at the front and read: "Balloon Pilot Licence – Valid for all Free-Flying Balloons".

'I'm a balloon pilot!' I said elatedly. 'I'm really and truly a balloon pilot!'

XI
LAUNCHING THE SKYLARK

Ordering a new hot-air balloon was an exciting and unique experience. I spent an evening with Simon and Laura to look at Cameron's brochures and to consider the various options and accessories that were available. I had long since decided that I wanted the so-called Seven, a 77,000 cubic foot sports model like the Pumpkin. It was designed to carry a maximum of four people – pilot plus three passengers – and as I was intending to specialize in flights for two, it would suit my purposes perfectly. Its flying characteristics would be ideal at all temperatures and I wouldn't have to worry about overloading.

'You can have a balloon made from scratch,' Simon explained enthusiastically. 'That way you can have it done to your exact specifications with your own colours and designs and anything you want written on it.'

'That would be great,' I said, 'but there are so many colour samples and designs to choose from.' As I paged through the brochure, I noticed a selection of half-a-dozen attractive balloons on one page that seemed to have more reasonable prices. 'What are these, then?' I asked. 'These prices aren't too bad.'

Simon took the brochure from me, and adjusting his glasses, he checked the fine print, comparing the prices with those on the official price list. 'These are ready-made balloons,' he said.

'They're a couple of thousand dollars cheaper because they're all ready to go. You could purchase one of these if you like, but you'd have no choice of colour or design. It's up to you. I'm sure they're still available.'

Over the next two hours all the decisions were made. I decided on a ready-made balloon aptly named Golden Delicious, a colourfully designed envelope made up of yellow, light green, dark green, white and black. The luxurious Cameron basket would come with green suede trim, and I picked out top-of-the-range burners, propane fuel tanks, hyperlast top, and a host of optional extras. This was going to be a wonderful balloon and I was anxious to get my order in to ensure the fastest possible dispatch.

One advantage of buying the ready-made Golden Delicious envelope was that it would speed up delivery, allowing me to get my new company organized for the summer ahead. If Simon could phone my order in to England right away I could have my own balloon all ready to go in two or three weeks, and my business would finally take off – literally! I could see my advertising now – "Flights for Two". Even better, I thought, "Romantic Flights for Two!" All I needed now was a name for my new balloon company, and I knew at least one person I could ask for ideas.

I hadn't spoken to Peter Broderick for a few weeks. We'd both been busy with school-related activities, and I'd been engrossed with ballooning, trying to get my training finished off. We hadn't had much time for socializing so it was a pleasant change to meet at the Black Dog and catch up on a few things. He was surprised to hear that I had finished everything and was now a fully qualified balloon pilot with a balloon on the way.

'Well, congratulations!' he said excitedly. 'I knew you'd do it. I don't seem to have your tenacity and endurance – too many things competing for my attention. But I did win the Duffins Creek squash tournament!'

We chatted for a while about one thing and another and eventually I brought up the matter of my new balloon company. 'I'm definitely going ahead with this idea,' I told him. 'As soon as my balloon arrives from England I'm going to get things organized, and I'll be taking paying passengers this summer. I've spent a fortune on the balloon, and I still have to buy a chase vehicle and trailer, as well as an inflator fan and other accessories. I'll have to start getting some of my investment back as soon as I can.'

Peter empathized with me, realizing that the investment was considerable. He was also all too aware that the original plan would have had us sharing the expense, relieving me of the financial burden of paying for everything myself. 'What will you do about crew?' he asked, leaning forward heavily on the table.

'I'll have to find some crew,' I said. 'I'll need at least one good chaser. Apart from that, most balloonists seem to get passengers involved, and if they're keen to help, I think that's a good idea.'

'You know you can always count on me to help out – and you won't have to pay me.'

'Well, yes, of course. That would be great, especially as you have some ballooning experience. How would you feel about being the chief chaser?'

'Sounds good to me. It seems like an enjoyable, straightforward job.'

I thought about my first experience chasing the balloon and Simon's extra efforts to make it challenging and interesting. Peter, I thought, would make a great chaser. He had a way of dealing with people, especially when they were angry or upset, and he would be very useful in awkward or difficult situations. 'That's that, then,' I told him. 'You can be the chaser.'

As we left the Black Dog and walked over to our cars I remembered that I needed a name for my new balloon company and I wanted to ask Peter for any ideas or suggestions. 'I need something catchy,' I told him, 'something that says it all. See if you can think of an idea. Think in terms of romantic flights into blue yonder.'

'Leave it with me,' he said as he climbed into his car. 'I'll give it some thought over the next few days.' Giving a quick thumbs-up sign, he slammed the creaky door of his well-used car and drove off.

I had plenty to occupy myself with over the next three weeks. I had seen a marvellous vehicle on display at a local dealership in Duffins Creek. It seemed to be everything I was looking for in terms of the ideal chase vehicle and I needed to check it out.

I stopped one day to take a closer look, and it didn't take the salesman long to convince me that I need look no further. It was a white Ram Charger, shiny brand new with every optional extra. The four-wheel drive system was exceptionally convenient and easy to handle, and with the over-sized wheels I knew there'd be little chance of getting stuck in muddy fields. It was an expensive purchase, but with some negotiation and a willingness to trade in my Buick, we soon had a deal and the Ram Charger was mine.

It seemed strange driving to school in my new transportation, but it was a pleasure to drive: smooth, powerful and – air-conditioned! Students and staff alike admired it and parents seemed to be intrigued. The curious expressions on their faces seemed to be asking, 'Who is this principal who four wheels it to school in a Ram Charger?'

Over the next few days I managed to find a suitable trailer as well. It was custom made by a local mechanic, and although smaller than I would have liked, it was quite big enough to hold all my equipment, including the bulky inflation fan that I'd ordered from Quebec. All I needed now was my new balloon.

It was three weeks to the day since I'd ordered my balloon when I received the news. I'd just finished dealing with a difficult situation involving a conflict between two parents when I was called back to my office for an important phone call. 'The lady said it was urgent,' Terri advised me as I came in.

Laura's voice caught me off guard. 'Hi,' she said. 'Have I got news for you!'

'Laura! It's you. What's so urgent?'

'I'm calling to let you know your balloon is in this country.'

It was welcome news, but as I had been expecting it any day, it was no big surprise. 'That's fantastic,' I said. 'Has it been delivered to your place?'

'No, it hasn't. It's at the airport and there's a mountain of red tape to work through before they can release it. It comes under

"Importing Foreign Aircraft", so you can imagine; it'll take at least three days before we can get it out of there.'

'Three days! How can I wait three more days?'

Laura laughed. 'Never mind,' she said. 'I do have some other good news as well. I have something for you. Will you be there if I come down to your school right now?'

'Of course. What have you got?'

'Wait and see. I'll be there in forty-five minutes.'

Laura arrived some time later carrying a large shopping bag.

'We were allowed to take some of the items away as they are not strictly part of the balloon,' she beamed, 'so I thought you'd like to have them today.'

She unloaded the bag onto my desk and excitedly went through the items one by one. 'Look at this,' she exclaimed like a little girl on her birthday. 'Your personal flight bag, matching the green suede trim on the basket. Special compartment for your logbook and licence. Space for your emergency lighters, gloves, maps, everything…'

Laura's enthusiasm was very catching and it was wonderful to receive all the brand new balloon accessories, from the state-of-the-art instrument package to the emergency drop line and a couple of spare karabiners. At least I'd have something to take home, and I could look forward to taking delivery of the balloon a few days later.

I received another phone call that evening. This time it was from Peter who breathlessly told me he'd come up with some ideas about a name for my new company. 'I've been giving it a lot of thought,' he said excitedly. 'I've got two ideas that I'm sure you'll find interesting.'

'I hope so,' I told him, 'because everything I've thought of so far has been eminently unsatisfactory!'

'Well, how about this? Since balloons are so tied up with wind and weather, and they'll only go where the wind takes them, how about "Gone With the Wind" as the name of your balloon business?' Peter was obviously enthused about this name and quite pleased with himself for thinking of it. I instantly hated it!

'It's catchy, all right. But it's not really what I had in mind. Too much like Scarlet O'Hara and I don't give a damn sort of thing. I really want something that contains the word balloons.'

Peter seemed disappointed at my reaction, but he proceeded to explain his second idea, hoping I would find it more agreeable. 'When I was a kid,' he said reflectively, 'we used to talk about doing things for a lark or a laugh – a fun sort of thing. You could think of taking off in a balloon as a bit of a lark. A lark in the sky or a sky lark. And also the bird, the skylark, is known for flying at great heights, soaring for hours in the early morning and before sunset in the evening, just like balloons do. So how about Skylark Balloons? That would be a great name for a balloon company that takes romantic couples for a lark in the sky. What do you think?'

'Bingo! My God,' I said, 'you've hit the nail on the head; that's absolutely perfect. That's exactly what I've been looking for; Skylark Balloons – yes! That's it!'

'Well, there you are, then.' Peter was obviously pleased that his second idea had been so well received, and he was glad to be a part of the decision making, even though he was no longer directly involved. Everything was done now. I just needed my gentle giant and Skylark Balloons would be in business.

By the end of the week the red tape had been dealt with and Simon and Laura were ready to go through their delivery procedure. I thought they would have simply called and said the balloon was ready to be picked up, but no such thing. They had a delivery process that rivalled that of any new car sale, and they picked a pleasant evening in May to take me through it.

'We'll meet you at the Glasgow launch site about six o'clock,' Simon told me when he phoned that morning with a satisfied tone to his voice. 'We'll have everything ready for you.'

It was one of those evenings that balloon pilots look forward to – no surface wind to speak of and all the cumulus clouds rapidly dissipating to make way for a clear, blue evening sky. Naomi and I arrived at the site in the Ram Charger about 6 p.m. as agreed, pulling the new trailer painted with its specially chosen colours – green with black trim to match the balloon – and containing my new inflation fan. Simon's truck was already there. Sitting

112

proudly on his trailer was the magnificent new basket with its green suede trim and a sturdy green canvas balloon bag containing the new envelope, all ready to go.

'The new balloon owner!' Laura announced as we pulled into the field. The two of them walked over and led us to their trailer where they proudly showed off the new equipment. 'You are now the registered owner of a unique aircraft,' Simon told me. 'Voila! You're new balloon!'

'That is amazing,' I said, rather more calmly than the occasion deserved. 'Thanks so much.'

Laura looked at me in utter astonishment with wide eyes and open mouth. 'That's it? Aren't you over the moon with excitement and exhilaration? I thought you'd be jumping up and down! You should have seen me when I got my new balloon. They couldn't hold me down for a week!'

I was thrilled at finally receiving my balloon, of course, but my enthusiasm was temporally dampened at the thought of how much money I had invested in it. How would I ever recover that investment conducting balloon flights for two? Perhaps I would, but it would take a very long time.

Over the next hour I became thoroughly engrossed in the experience of being introduced to my new free-flying aircraft and any financial preoccupations were soon forgotten. We set up the basket first, carefully installing the pristine burners and zipping up the luxurious suede trim on the uprights. The four propane tanks had to be strapped into place in the corners of the basket, which we anchored to the ground with three tether ropes that Simon had brought along for that purpose.

Finally, we came to the balloon envelope. The smell of newness and the feel of the smooth fabric was thrilling in itself. The top third of the envelope was made with special flame-resistant hyperlast material, an exceptionally tough fabric that was virtually indestructible. We worked together, stretching out the envelope on the ground, attaching the flying wires to the basket and burner frames, and finally dragging the fan into place to begin the cold inflation. Simon handled the crown line for me as the envelope quickly expanded before the powerful blast of cold air. The full beauty of the colours and design were portrayed as we stretched out the material, creating an enormous, sun-drenched cavern, glowing magically in the evening sunlight. I was tempted to enter, but resisted doing so, afraid to leave any boot prints on my precious new balloon.

I finally positioned myself in the basket and prepared myself to complete the hot inflation. The powerful burners were smooth and easy to handle, and in a very short time the envelope rose majestically over the basket, proudly showing itself off to the world for the very first time. It was a magnificent sight! Laura, of course, was as excited as ever, and she and Naomi held the basket down until Simon brought the end of the crown line to me so I could clip it into place. 'What's her name?' he asked, leaning heavily on the side of the basket. 'Have you named her yet?'

I smiled contentedly and blasted the burners to create some buoyancy. 'I have, indeed,' I told him. 'Her name is Skylark. Bless all who fly in her!'

'Skylark! That's a great name. Very apt too. Here we go, then. The Skylark is launched!'

They removed their weight from the basket and the Skylark slowly rose to the end of her tethers – her first time off the ground. This prompted a resounding cheer from the three spectators, reminding me of my first time in a balloon on the edge of the Yorkshire Dales, but this time it was my very own balloon. It would have been wonderful to reach for the sky then and there and float off across the peaceful countryside. But this was not the time. Such flights were ahead of me in abundance and I could wait.

It was an exciting hour that followed, and although tethering can be so boring to a keen pilot, I enjoyed trying her out, taking Naomi and Laura in turns to rise fifty feet in the air before gently descending to the ground. Simon declined the invitation. 'I've been in a balloon before,' he said wryly. Tethered ballooning was definitely not his thing.

Eventually, as the sun sank below the horizon, we reluctantly deflated the Skylark and packed her away. But it was a satisfying drive home. Here was I, a qualified balloon pilot with my own balloon and an exciting business ahead of me. 'Any romantic passengers out there can give me a call now,' I told Naomi. 'I'm ready and waiting for them.'

The Skylark's maiden flight took place from Mount Albert a few days later on a glorious Sunday morning. Peter was supposed to be my official chaser, but he flew with me that first time. We brought a few friends along to see us off with the customary cheer, and between them they figured out how to chase a balloon as well. Not surprisingly, Simon was at the site with a group of passengers too, and the two balloons took off together, following a similar flight path and landing fifteen miles downwind within sight of each other. The champagne flowed freely, of course, along with the exuberant and boisterous behaviour needed to mark such an auspicious occasion.

This was our pattern for the next few weeks. As Laura had firmly told me, 'Your balloon isn't just for business, you know. Make sure you have plenty of fun with it as well.'

I followed her advice until the middle of July, when I placed some pertinent ads around town and in some local papers, looking for both passengers and crew. Skylark Balloons was in business now, but that wasn't the end of the fun by any means. In fact, it was just the beginning.

XII
NEW CREW AND WINDLESS WEATHER

The phone was ringing with a strange, unusual tone and I rushed to answer, only to find no one there – yet it kept on ringing. It suddenly dawned on me. This was the new Skylark Balloons phone with its defective, whiny tone telling me that I had my first potential customer. By the time I'd fumbled with the two telephones on my desk and connected my ear to the right one, the caller was ready to hang up.

'Skylark Balloons,' I gushed breathlessly. 'How can I help you?'

After a moment of silence, the caller hesitatingly explained his call. 'Er…I noticed an ad in a local store in Duffins Creek saying you were looking for crew. I just wondered what you need exactly. I'm very interested and I'd love to get involved.'

Another Englishman, I thought, noting the London accent. Can't be bad.

'Yes,' I told him, 'we are looking for crew, and if you live here in Duffins Creek, so much the better. Do you know anything about balloons?'

'Nothing at all, but I'm a rugby player from England, and I thought you could probably use someone who could lift heavy equipment.' He laughed cautiously.

I thought of Big John who crewed for Alan Crossland and how useful someone like that would be. Although I knew nothing about the caller, something told me he'd be worth interviewing. We chatted briefly and he seemed like a genuine, quiet-spoken man. 'Do you know the Black Dog pub?' I asked him. 'If you could meet me there later this evening, I can tell you more about it and we'll see where it leads.'

The meeting at the Black Dog was highly successful. The man's name was Tom Dale, a civil engineer working in the Toronto area. He wasn't nearly as big as Big John, but he was certainly a strapping, healthy fellow with a quiet sense of humour and an easy manner, and he seemed to be keenly interested in learning about balloons. I had no hesitation in taking him on. Although I didn't realize it then, that first meeting, besides giving me a capable and dedicated right hand man, was the beginning of a ten-year friendship as well.

'I can't pay you,' I told him right away. 'Balloon pilots offer chasers and crew a chance to learn and to be involved in an exciting and unusual activity. The thrill of working around balloons, meeting interesting people and taking the occasional free balloon flight is your reward, so you'll have to decide if that's sufficient.'

'That's what I'm looking for,' Tom insisted earnestly. 'I've seen hot-air balloons flying north of Toronto, and I'm quite fascinated with them. I'm getting too old for rugby now and I need a new activity. Ballooning seems to be the kind of exciting sport I need right at the moment.'

Tom turned out to be the ideal crewman and I couldn't have hoped to find anyone better. I knew I could count on Peter being available from time to time, but I felt Tom would always be there. He showed an interest and fascination with balloons that rivalled my own. His chance to show his colours came soon after that first meeting.

Within the next few days, several calls came in on my whiny balloon phone looking for information about the cost of taking a flight and other details about what was involved. Two flights were booked almost immediately and I asked Tom along so he could start getting some practical experience and learn about the tricky art of chasing. I was delighted to see that he took to it like a duck to water.

It felt strange to be taking paying passengers at first, but over the next few weeks it became almost routine. Peter and Tom made a good team, crewing and chasing together, and on some occasions, when Peter wasn't available, Tom started to do the job on his own. This gave him the confidence he needed, and before long I considered him my chief crewman.

One morning towards the end of summer, we were waiting for our passengers, Jim and Maureen, who had arranged to meet us in Duffins Creek. It was a glorious day with extremely light winds, and in the cool early morning air a feeling of exhilaration and excitement swept over the three of us as we anticipated the morning's flight. Tom looked at the blue, cloudless sky as he leaned against the trailer with his arms tightly folded. 'Those lucky people,' he said to Peter, shaking his head. 'They're in for a fantastic flight this morning.'

'It should be an interesting flight path too,' I yawned, still trying to wake up. 'We're taking off from Glasgow again. I guess it's about time you had a flight, eh Tom?'

Tom perked up at the suggestion. 'Just tell me when!'

'We'll have to work it out soon. As you know, I only take two passengers – I like to leave a safety margin and keep the weight down.'

Jim and Maureen arrived within a few minutes. They were a pleasant, middle-aged couple, but I could tell from the start that Maureen was apprehensive about the whole thing, and I wondered if her obvious nervousness would subside before we reached Glasgow. Despite charming efforts by Peter, she had little to say during the thirty-minute drive. She clung tightly to her husband's hand, staring dreamily out of the window. By the time I drove into the abandoned school site at Glasgow she had firmly made up her mind.

'I'm not going,' she announced, climbing gingerly out of the Ram. 'I'll die of shock if I go up in that thing.'

No amount of coaxing and reassurance from her husband could change her mind, and Jim, rather embarrassed, shrugged his shoulders and looked at us, almost begging for a solution to his dilemma. 'Sorry,' he said. 'I think we'll have to forget it.'

'But you want to fly, don't you?' I asked him.

'Certainly I do. I'm dead keen on it.'

'Well, no problem then. Maureen can travel in the truck with the crew, and you and I can fly in the balloon. How does that sound?'

'Well, it sounds great, if Maureen doesn't mind.'

Maureen looked highly relieved, and for the first time she relaxed as if a great weight had been lifted from her shoulders. 'You go ahead,' she beamed. 'I know you want to.'

Tom coughed and looked at me quizzically. 'Any chance...?' he mumbled. 'You know...'

'Oh, of course. Why not. Here's a good opportunity for you.' I turned to Jim and told him with the utmost sincerity and conviction, 'Tom will be our co-pilot today!'

Although this news made no impression whatsoever on our passenger, it almost caused major convulsions in Tom who reminded me, between coughs and wheezes, that he couldn't be the co-pilot, because he'd never been in a balloon before in his entire life.

We rose slowly and gently into a clear blue sky and we were treated to the magnificent vistas of farms, lakes and forest that I had seen so many times before. The wind was remarkably calm, perhaps two or three knots, and I knew we wouldn't travel very far. But Tom and Jim were completely awestruck. I quickly ascended to 1000 feet and then more slowly to 3000 feet and more to give them a chance to see the distant views. They admired Lake Ontario and the city of Toronto to the south and lake Simcoe to the north, amazed at the stillness and calm as we floated so slowly along.

If Tom had been keen before, I knew this experience would hook him for life as it had done me. I could see a similar thought process going through his head.

'This is quite incredible,' he muttered softly. 'I should learn how to fly one of these myself.'

Jim and Tom excitedly compared their thoughts on distant views, trying to identify towns and villages, rivers and lakes.

The time past quickly and I started to think about returning to earth. We'd been in the air for more than an hour. I was surprised to see that we had travelled only four or five miles and we were hanging over thick forest making very little progress in any direction. 'We'll have to think about landing soon,' I informed my two captivated passengers. 'I'd better contact Peter.'

'Skylark to Ram.' The radio crackled into life.

'Reading you, Skylark. Come in.'

'Peter, we're looking to land at the first opportunity. Are you with us?'

'We've been sitting at the side of the road here for half an hour. I can see you just fine, but you don't seem to be going anywhere.'

'We're out of wind,' I told him. 'I'm coming down low to see if I can find some. Stay with us.'

'I'll keep you in sight. Over and out.'

I allowed the Skylark to fall gently towards the treetops below. It took a few minutes, but it was like a smooth elevator all the way. Soon we were a mere ten feet above the forest and we could see the thick undergrowth below us, but still we were going nowhere. It seemed too calm and peaceful to be worried. Tom and Jim joked about having to land on the treetops, quite convinced that I'd find a way out, but I began to see landing in the forest as a real possibility. 'This is a very unusual condition,' I told them confidently. 'In all the flights I've done in a balloon, I've never once been becalmed like this. I'm going up high again to see if I can somehow get clear of the forest.'

Rising back to 3000 feet was easy enough, but the problem was fuel consumption. Technically, the four tanks allowed for about two hours flying time, but we'd been in the air for an hour and a half now, and the quick ascent used up most of the remaining fuel. I still couldn't find any wind.

Tom and Jim had become strangely quiet now. 'This patch of forest below us is only about two miles across,' I observed. 'See the fields and meadows beyond? They'd make perfect landing spots, but I have no way of reaching them.' They began to understand the predicament.

'So what happens if we can't move away?' Jim asked, becoming more concerned now.

'If the worst comes to the worst, I'll have to land in the trees. We won't be hurt but my balloon will be in an awful mess. In fact it'll be ripped to shreds! And God knows how we'll get everything out to the road.'

I shaded my eyes and looked for detail in all directions. I could see my white Ram Charger parked on a side road at the edge of the forest, so I knew I had radio contact when needed. As I looked, I noticed a narrow laneway that seemed to lead from the truck all the way into the forest. 'Look at that,' I said to Tom, pointing it out. 'Where does that laneway lead? It seems to come all the way in.'

'There's a house of some kind right below us,' he said, straining his eyes to see. 'That's one heck of a long driveway.'

I knew it was my only chance. We were exactly above the house that seemed to have a green lawn the size of a postage stamp in front of it, and though there wasn't much chance of hitting it, at least we'd be in a rescuable position if we landed in the trees. I called Peter immediately.

'Peter, I'm coming down. Drive into the forest to the end of the laneway you can see on your left.'

'Understood. I'm on my way.'

Now I knew why I'd learned how to do a cold descent under Simon's direction. I let the Skylark cool and we began to fall rapidly. I needed to reach the ground quickly before any hint of wind blew us off course, and to my amazement, it worked like a charm. At 1000 feet I burned furiously to slow the descent. We continued falling, more controlled now, but straight and true until, incredibly, the Skylark landed gently and smoothly in the centre of the soft, green lawn. As I carefully feathered the burners to maintain inflation, the Ram reached us, and Peter was there immediately to hold us down. Everything was under perfect control.

'How on earth did you do that?' Tom asked in utter amazement.

I checked my last propane fuel tank. It was completely empty. 'Just don't ask me to do it again,' I said. 'It was pure luck!'

Skylark Balloons quickly came into its own during that first exciting summer. Through word of mouth and limited advertising we were able to get all the passengers we could handle, and by fall my whiny balloon phone was ringing constantly.

Peter was now heavily involved in marathon running, though he still made time for chasing on occasion, but Tom had become my steadfast crewman and chaser. We realized that we would need more help. We wanted crewmen who'd be keenly interested, dedicated and reliable. An unexpected phone call one morning gave me the opportunity I was looking for.

'We want to offer a hot-air balloon trip as first prize in our competition,' the man told me. It was the local press calling, and they'd seen my advertising on the pages of their own newspaper.

'That sounds like a great idea,' I responded. 'Would you like me to make up a gift certificate for the occasion? You could simply purchase it and present it to the winner.'

It seemed like a good way to handle it and we quickly agreed on the details. Over the following month the competition ran its course and the certificate was duly presented. A local firefighter in Duffins Creek by the name of Sean McLellan won the balloon trip for two, and Tom and I arranged to meet him and his girlfriend on a beautiful October afternoon. As expected, we found the couple eagerly looking forward to finding out what ballooning was all about.

'I can't believe I won this trip,' Sean told us as we introduced ourselves and exchanged the usual pleasantries. 'This is my girlfriend, Carol. We've been talking about it for the past week.'

'Well, congratulations!' I said, shaking his hand. 'You've got the perfect evening for it. Have you been in a balloon before?'

'Neither of us have. It's a totally new experience, but I've often wondered what balloon flying was like. Do you use helium?'

'Not at all! It's a hot-air balloon. We use hot air.'

Sean showed a great interest in the balloon itself. He had many questions and he seemed to take in the information with great fascination and delight. 'I've never seen a balloon close up before. What an amazing craft!'

Wind conditions were very favourable and we were able to launch from the lakeside in Duffins Creek itself. Sean was pleased with this, as he particularly wanted to see the fire station from the air, especially if any of his co-workers were there to watch the balloon as it crossed town.

It was a successful and rewarding flight. The four of us lingered over champagne, reluctant to go home after an exhilarating adventure, and Tom and I felt that Sean was already becoming one of us. He had enthusiastically thrown himself into the spirit of ballooning, anxious to learn every small detail and marvelling at the simple ingenuity of the Skylark's construction.

'Is there any way I can get involved in this?' he asked eagerly as we prepared to leave.

'You'd be very welcome to come along with us any time,' I told him. 'We fly all year round, winter and summer, and we're looking for crew all the time. I'll give you a call next time we fly.'

Sean seemed delighted with this. He joined us on the following weekend, and over a few weeks and months he became a dedicated crewman and chaser, passionately interested in his new endeavour. Like Tom, he was anxious to take every opportunity for leaving the ground, and though these opportunities didn't arise very often, he did manage to fly on occasion. By the spring, Sean was one of us – an indisputable part of Skylark Balloons.

When our early morning flights were done, we tended to spend some time at one of the many country restaurants that we came across on our way home. One morning, as we sipped Country Style's hot coffee, Sean told us how his love of balloons was making an impression on his family. 'My brother, Fergus, has been enviously listening to my balloon stories for weeks now,' he told us. 'He's becoming as keen as I am. If you could use more help, he'd love to join us sometime.'

'Why not? Bring him along if he's keen. In fact, you should tell him to phone me sometime.'

'Not only that,' Sean went on, shaking his finger in the air, 'we have a mutual friend, Mark Bacilli, who's just as intrigued with the idea. I can tell you, these guys are dynamite. Would you like to talk to Mark as well?'

Things were really moving along. I looked at Sean, amused at his uncontrolled fascination with hot-air balloons and his eagerness to involve others. 'If I have four dedicated guys who can do a good job crewing and chasing, I'll be more than satisfied,' I told him. 'If Fergus and Mark are as good as you say, let's try them out.'

Fergus and Mark turned out to be formidable crewmen, and I felt extremely fortunate to have found such dedicated and reliable men to be part of my team. As time went by, the five of us became firm friends, sharing exciting times with the fascinating characters we met on every flight, and participating in some hilarious and memorable events that would last us a lifetime.

By the second summer, the business was on a new course. We were becoming known far and wide, and the word was out that there was only one place to call for a romantic flight for two – and that was Skylark Balloons.

XIII
PREPOSTEROUS PROPOSALS AND LOVE SICK LOSERS

'I was wondering… do you have a balloon shaped like a nude woman?'

The question stumped me for a moment as I tried to take in what was being asked. My balloon phone had become an instrument of unexpected amusement lately, as the questions and requests became more and more bizarre.

'Not exactly,' I said politely. 'What do you have in mind?'

'Well, you see,' the woman went on with some hesitation and slight embarrassment in her voice, 'it's my husband's birthday next week, and I thought it would be quite funny to give him something like that. He gets a laugh out of that sort of thing.'

'I think you might have called the wrong company. Where did you find our number?'

'In the Yellow Pages, under Balloons.'

'Ah, well, you see, our balloons are the kind that take passengers into the sky. What you need is a place that sells party balloons. They might have what you're looking for.'

I laughed to myself as I hung up the phone. What next, I thought. It had only been the previous week when a young lady with stars in her eyes had explained her elaborate wedding plans and how the balloon would complete the romantic picture.

'I want you to have the balloon ready when we come out of church,' she gushed enthusiastically. 'As people throw confetti at us and cheer us on, we'll run down the walkway, jump into the basket, and you can fly off with us to the hotel where the reception is being held.'

I had to explain to her. 'The chance of pulling that one off is absolute zero. First of all, balloons can't be steered, so I can't take you anywhere the wind doesn't want to go. And secondly, the church is in Duffins Creek, so if the wind happens to be from the north that day we'll head straight for Lake Ontario.'

She was disappointed, of course, but I must have missed news of the latest trend-setting fad, because after that, romance and balloons seemed to be inexplicably tied together. In particular, I started to receive many enquiries about the possibility of getting engaged in the Skylark.

These requests were mostly from amorous young men who thought it would be the ultimate in romantic behaviour if they proposed marriage to their girlfriends in a hot-air balloon.

The first request for a balloon engagement came from a young local dentist by the name of Rod Barrington. He had set up a new dental practice in town the previous year and now felt he was in a position to get engaged in style. He came to chat with me personally to see what could be arranged. 'It must be a balloon for just the two of us,' he insisted. 'I don't want any other passengers in the balloon with us.'

'Of course, I understand,' I told him. 'We specialize in flights for two, but you'll have to get used to the idea that I'll be there, hearing every word you say.'

'Yes…,' he said wistfully. 'I suppose that can't be avoided.'

Rod was a nice enough fellow, but he gave the impression of being a bit full of himself and he clearly believed that his girlfriend was very lucky to land such a catch.

'What's your girlfriend's name?' I asked.

'Vicki. She's my dental hygienist at the practice. We've been dating for about a year.'

'Oh, so you work together. That's great!' I couldn't resist the chance to tease him a little. 'But what will you do if she says no to your proposal?'

Rod looked at me astounded and not a little insulted at my question.

'I can tell you this with absolute certainty,' he said, shaking his finger at me. 'There's no bloody way she'll say no!'

I thought it must be nice to be so confident. Rod settled the payment immediately, explaining that he was quite methodical and liked to have everything properly settled ahead of time.

Tom and Fergus were available to crew for the engagement flight and I told them about the special circumstances, warning them not to give anything away to Vicki while we were setting up.

'Rod is quite a serious guy,' I told them. 'He'll be furious if you let the cat out of the bag.'

I didn't need to worry. All the preparations went smoothly and we met Rod and Vicki in Duffins Creek according to plan on a calm, sunny afternoon. We had discovered a new launch site in Leaskdale, which was ideally located to give us a southerly flight path over some particularly beautiful countryside containing several small lakes and rivers. I planned to fly fairly low, emphasizing the romantic nature of the flight.

'I couldn't believe it when Rod said we were going on a balloon flight,' Vicki told us more than once. 'I'm just so excited about it. I never would have believed I'd be doing something like this.'

'You'll get a great view of Lake Ontario and the city,' Fergus said enviously as he set up the fan for inflation. He looked quickly at me as if to ask when it would be his turn to fly.

'Don't worry, Fergus. Your turn will come.'

I went through the usual safety routine with my romantic passengers, making sure they'd be ready for a hard landing if the wind speed increased. The two of them were thrilled as Tom and Mark waved us off, and like anyone flying in a balloon for the first time, they were astonished at the smooth ascent and the quiet gentleness of the flight.

It was an enjoyable balloon flight like the many others I had done, and I relaxed a little as the passengers excitedly admired the scenery and the many familiar landmarks in our flight path. At the halfway mark I gave Rod a knowing look, indicating that if he was going to propose, he'd better get on with it. He took my drift and, suddenly, things began to happen.

'Vicki,' he announced confidently. 'There's something I have to say.' He fished in his pocket and withdrew a small ring box, which he kept hidden in his hand. 'I want to do this properly.'

To my utter amazement the ardent suitor then fell down on his knees. Not a good idea, I thought, given the restricted space in the basket, but I shifted my position to accommodate his bulky feet.

Whoooosh! I saw his lips moving but the sound of the burner blast completely drowned out whatever he said.

Vicki seemed to have no idea what was going on. 'Rod, what on earth are you doing?'

'Vicki, I'm trying to…' Whoooosh! I had no option but to burn again. The balloon needed heat and I had to keep it flying safely no matter what. Besides, I was quite enjoying myself prolonging the proposal as much as possible.

Rod finally managed to get the words out uninterrupted. 'Vicki, what I'm trying to say is, will you marry me?'

He obviously knew his girl and she reacted exactly as he had predicted. 'Oh, Rod!' she exclaimed wildly, 'of course I'll marry you!'

Vicki leaned forward in an attempt to embrace him, but in the confined space she lost her footing and fell over him instead. The two of them ended up in an inelegant heap at my feet like a couple of amateur wrestlers.

'Now just a minute,' I said good naturedly, 'a proposal is one thing, but…'

The newly engaged couple struggled to get up from the floor and the three of us broke into wild laughter as we tried to return to some semblance of restraint. I had to put safety first and I focussed my attention once more on flying the balloon.

'I guess you said yes?' Rod enquired, now hugging Vicki and still laughing after the unconventional proposal. Suddenly he stopped and became quite serious. 'The ring!' he exclaimed. 'I've lost the ring!'

The two of them were suddenly back on their hands and knees searching for the ring box, which had been thrown aside in the confusion. It was quickly found, lodged behind one of the fuel tanks, much to Rod's relief. 'Thank God,' he said. 'It's worth a fortune.'

Rod dutifully placed the ring on Vicki's finger and they spent the rest of the flight in a close embrace, happily watching the pastoral world go by below them. We landed smoothly in a freshly cut hay field, dodging the huge bales as if by magic, and coming to rest close to the access gate on the far side.

Within minutes, Tom and Fergus were driving through to join us. They knew that congratulations were in order, and once we had packed the balloon away we spent some time celebrating with the strawberries and champagne that we'd brought along. I felt content, knowing that we'd made this couple happy and feeling that our first engagement flight had been highly successful. I looked forward to many more.

~

The word soon spread around and Skylark Balloons was asked to conduct many engagement flights over the following weeks and months. These were truly romantic flights for two and my crewmen and I enjoyed them thoroughly. We met dozens of interesting young couples, many of them professional people in the fields of medicine, law and education, and all of them fascinating and different in their own way.

I witnessed proposals of all kinds, some formal with impressive quotes and lines of poetry, and others casual and matter-of-fact. Some were pathetic pleas made on bended knee, and others were magnanimous offers of marriage to girls who were supposed to consider themselves lucky.

'How many proposals have you actually heard?' Tom asked me early one morning as we celebrated yet another engagement in a sun-bathed hay field.

'I've lost count,' I told him. 'But I can tell you this – I've heard more proposals than Elizabeth Taylor! I never realized there were so many exciting ways of proposing marriage.'

Our engagement flights were inevitably elating and invigorating. A trip in a hot-air balloon is in itself thrilling, but when a newly engaged couple is thrown into the mix it creates a wonderful atmosphere of excitement and celebration. We found this to be the case every time – with one exception. Inadvertently, we became involved in a planned engagement flight that seemed to spell disaster from the start.

Simon Wills called me one afternoon to see if I could help him with a flight booking he'd just made. 'I have a guy here – Jason – who's determined to propose to a young lady in a hot-air balloon,' he said. 'He wants a balloon just for the two of them but, as you know, I can't do that. My balloons are for eight passengers and I can't leave six empty spaces when people are waiting for flights.'

'So you want me to take them?'

'That's right, but he insists on flying with Northern Balloon Adventures. He won't phone you or anyone else, even though I've quoted him double price to fly with us. Maybe you could work for me on this one flight?'

'I don't see why not. I'll use my balloon and fly for you. You can pay me the usual cost of a flight for two.'

'Perfect! It's a deal then.'

It seemed a bit odd that Jason was willing to pay Simon double price rather than phone Skylark Balloons directly, I thought, but he must have had his reasons. Maybe he thought Duffins Creek was too far away, not realizing that we all use the same sites.

I phoned Jason the next day to make arrangements. As Simon had mentioned, he was very insistent on following through with his plan. 'I don't care about the cost,' he said. 'I just want a private balloon for me and Janet. Simon Wills said he could arrange it.'

'That's right,' I assured him. 'I've spoken to Simon and he's assigned me for this flight. We can arrange a great engagement flight for you with a strawberries-and-champagne celebration and everything will be fine. We just need to fix a date.'

Jason seemed pleased with this and, after consulting with Janet, he called back to confirm. 'Everything's a go,' he told me. 'I just told her we're going on a balloon flight so she knows nothing about the proposal. Keep it under your hat.'

'Of course,' I said. 'You can trust us. We've done many engagement flights before.'

I met Tom and Sean at our usual meeting place in Duffins Creek the following Sunday morning. 'Where are the passengers?' Tom asked, glancing at the empty truck.

'I told you. They're meeting us in Stoneville. This is Simon's flight. Hop in.'

All my crew were experienced with engagement flights now and Tom and Sean eagerly looked forward to another celebration. 'There's something nagging me about this one,' I told them as we drove up to Stoneville. 'Jason seemed a little unsure of himself, and for some reason I don't understand, he's willingly paid double price. I hope he knows what he's doing.'

We met Jason and Janet at Simon's meeting place in Stoneville. They seemed like a normal couple, though Jason was considerably older and I got the impression that all the affection was coming from one side. 'We're really looking forward to this, aren't we, Janet?' The hopeful suitor was forcefully cheerful, and as we helped them into the back of the Ram Charger, he furtively took out a paper package from inside his shirt and secretly handed it to me.

'What's this?' I asked quietly.

'It's a long-stemmed red rose. Can you hide it somewhere in the balloon until I need it?'

'I'll try my best. I hope it won't get crushed along the way.'

We headed for the site at Mount Albert where Simon was already inflating in preparation for his morning flight. His passengers and crew were milling around, some helping while others stood back waiting. As Tom and Sean dragged out the envelope and started making preparations for our flight, Simon motioned me over to his balloon where he was about to light the burners.

'How's Jason?' he asked, as if expecting bad news.

'He's fine. They seem like a regular couple. I'm not expecting any problem.'

'That's good, then. As long as they're happy. See you in the air.'

Jason and Janet were intrigued as they watched Simon and his passengers take to the air amid plenty of hoopla and excitement. They'd obviously never seen anything like it. 'We're next,' Jason told his girlfriend enthusiastically, placing an affectionate arm around her shoulders. They watched with great interest and excitement as the Skylark rose to its position over the basket, and then eagerly climbed in.

Simon's balloon had travelled three or four miles by the time the Skylark left the ground, but it was such an enormous size that it seemed much closer. For the first twenty minutes we followed a similar flight path and then, as I gained some altitude, we drifted off in a slightly different direction. I knew we'd land in separate locations, probably several miles apart.

I had hidden Jason's rose behind one of the propane tanks, still wrapped in its brown paper package. Janet was leaning on one side of the basket, quite content to admire the scenery and enjoy the tranquillity of gentle flight, when Jason moved in close to her. He motioned to me, indicating that he would like to have the rose now, so I carefully removed it from its package and passed it to him. Surprisingly, it was still intact.

'Janet,' he said gently, 'I know I haven't known you for long, but I feel you're everything to me. I have something for you.' He pulled the rose from behind his back and presented it to her.

'What's this?' she said, surprised at the flower's sudden appearance. She glanced at me over her shoulder, looking slightly embarrassed.

'It's a rose. But I have something else for you too.' He produced a ring from his pocket and took her left hand in his. 'Will you marry me, Janet?' Without waiting for an answer, Jason started to place the ring on his intended's finger, but she pulled away, agitated and annoyed.

'Are you out of your mind?' she snapped. 'What do you mean marry you? I hardly know you!'

If I'd had a parachute handy I would have cheerfully baled out then and there. But I had no escape. I was stuck firmly in the basket with them while they dealt with this tumultuous stage in their relationship. All I could do was burn intermittently to drown out the raised voices that ensued.

Jason was clearly hurt and upset. 'We've been going out for six months,' he said. 'Didn't you expect I'd be proposing to you?'

'No I did not! I've no intention of marrying you or anyone else for a long time yet.'

'So I've been wasting my time then?'

'If you were thinking of marriage, I guess you have.'

It went on and on until I called Tom on the radio to say we were landing soon. I could see the Ram on the road below, following us closely, and luckily, I found an open meadow close to an accessible gate and managed a fairly gentle landing.

I'd been desperately hoping the basket wouldn't tip in case it caused some unwanted togetherness. That was the last thing we needed, especially as the noisy argument had evolved into a stony silence just before we came in to land. Mercifully, the Ram rolled into the field almost as soon as we touched down, sparing me the burden of dealing with this alone. But the embarrassment wasn't over yet.

'Well, congratulations you two! How does it feel to be engaged?' Sean expected to find an excited and happy couple as he approached the still inflated Skylark, but instead he was greeted by two sad-eyed ex-lovers, the picture of misery. I wanted to sink through the floor at Sean's unfortunate greeting, but I just gave him an expressionless ogle and he quickly got the picture.

'Here,' I said. 'Take the crown line and let's deflate.'

The unhappy couple wasted no time in disembarking from the basket. Janet made a beeline for the truck and climbed into the back seat, slamming the door behind her. Her disillusioned ex-boyfriend silently watched us pack up, his hands pushed deeply in his pockets as he pondered his disastrous attempt to catch the girl of his dreams.

'Tough luck,' I said to him sympathetically. 'Don't take it to heart – these things don't always work out the way we expect.' I thought he was going to burst into tears and I quickly turned away.

We left him to his thinking and he seemed to cheer up a little by the time we'd finished.

'Did you say something about strawberries and champagne?' he asked as we finished loading up the trailer. 'I was looking forward to that.'

'It's all in the cooler. It's up to you.'

'Why not! Let's open the champagne.'

'What about Janet?'

'Nah…let her sulk on her own.'

Tom and Sean were only too pleased to oblige. They set up the small table at the end of the trailer and popped open a bottle of champagne. The strawberries had been on ice the whole time and they were fresh and juicy. Jason seemed to relax a little more and we all drank to his future, feeling rather sorry for him and understanding how he felt – from a man's point of view. I felt sorry for Janet. We needed a female crewmember to go and talk to her, but unfortunately none was available. She'd have to manage by herself for now.

The drive back to Stoneville was a little strained, to say the least, but Tom gallantly gave his place in the front passenger seat to Jason. This seemed to help and we made it back with no more outbursts. We watched them go their separate ways and then set off on our drive home to Duffins Creek.

'That was a little different,' Tom observed as we drove away. 'I wonder if they'll make up and maybe get married one day.'

'I don't suppose we'll ever know,' I said wryly, 'but somehow, I don't think so.'

XIV
ASHES TO ASHES AND SHORTHORN BULLS

The Oak Ridges Moraine is an irregular ridge of rolling hills stretching more than a hundred miles from east to west across southern Ontario. The effect of this unique land feature has been to create some exquisitely beautiful scenery, including many small lakes, high cliffs, spectacular lookout points and a number of popular ski resorts.

During the autumn months the natural beauty of the moraine is further enhanced by Ontario's famous fall colours, as the incredibly bright orange, red and yellow maple leaves blend with the luxurious dark green of Canadian pine. Not surprisingly, Skylark Balloons was always in big demand at that time of the year, as passengers eagerly made their bookings for our fall colour flights.

Each of our balloon trips was unique and special in its own way, but some flights stood out as being particularly memorable. One October, the fall colours and the moraine provided circumstances that led to two unforgettable trips, one highly embarrassing and the other downright scary.

The first of these started off innocently enough with a simple phone call.

'I particularly want to fly while the colours are at their best,' she told me adamantly. 'I know everyone calls you at this time of the year, but I hope you can accommodate me and my husband on an early morning flight. It's very important to us.'

She told me her name was Sheila, and it all sounded rather urgent. Norris, her husband, wasn't a keen flyer, but he'd promised to accompany her on this flight because it was something she had to do. And it had to be as soon as possible when the colours were at their peak, before the leaves started to wilt and die.

I assumed it was for their wedding anniversary. I had done many flights to celebrate special occasions, and anniversaries were among the most popular. I assured Sheila that we'd arrange an unforgettable flight for the two of them, and she could look forward to receiving confirmation the following week.

'Let's make this a really good experience for them,' I told Tom when I called him. 'I'll make up a champagne picnic they won't forget. Meanwhile, see if you can get in touch with Mark.'

Even the drive to Mount Albert was spectacular that morning. The sun appeared on the horizon and caught the brightly coloured maples, giving the appearance of thousands of tiny lights glowing in the trees. Tom and Mark chatted to our middle-aged passengers in the back of the Ram, telling them about the amazing scene they were going to witness from the air. Norris, in turn, asked them apprehensively about the safety of a balloon flight.

I joined in the conversation as I drove along. 'Balloon flight is the safest possible way to fly,' I assured him. 'Just think of the balloon as an enormous parachute. If anything went wrong, we'd simply float to the ground.'

This seemed to reassure him tremendously, and he turned his conversation and questions to other things, like the technical aspects of a balloon's structure. Once we reached our launch site, he showed great interest in the karabiners and flying wires, speculating about their strength and load limits. He seemed quite satisfied with his personal safety check and contented himself with watching the inflation and the final preparations for the flight.

136

'Does it all meet with your approval then, Norris?' I asked him, teasing him a little.

'Oh yes! I'm most impressed with the simplicity and strength of a craft like this. I've no reservations about flying in it at all.' He laughed nervously.

Most passengers are a little apprehensive when we first leave the ground, but they quickly settle down when they begin to experience the quiet tranquillity of balloon flight. Sheila and Norris were no exceptions.

'My goodness!' Sheila exclaimed as we rose high above the treetops. 'Have you ever seen such an awesome sight as that?'

A world of colour and contrast stretched out before us. The autumn leaves in the patches of woodland and forest below us glistened and sparkled under the morning sun, and the fields and meadows, now stripped of all their crops, formed a patchwork quilt in the distance. We were still low enough to hear the gurgling creeks and streams as they made their way to the lake. We came across the occasional deer and more rabbits than we could count. Perfect for an anniversary flight, I thought.

'I think we should stay low to appreciate the forest,' I told my passengers. 'Maybe we can go higher towards the end of the flight.'

'That sounds wonderful. I don't want to go too high, anyway.' Norris leaned into the long side of the basket, looking as relaxed as I thought he would ever be.

Sheila was quiet and pensive, drinking in the incredible beauty of the colourful vista before her. She was clearly at peace with herself, not worried or nervous in any way and obviously doing something she had dreamed about for a long time.

'You certainly picked the right time of the year,' I told her. 'Ballooning is wonderful in any season, but I think the fall offers something special.'

She smiled without replying and returned to her thoughtful dream.

As we neared the end of the wooded area I brought the balloon up to 1000 feet. I could see the open fields a mile or two ahead of us and I knew we would land in one of them. There was a country road to my right. I could see the Ram now as Tom drove along, keeping pace with the Skylark.

'About fifteen minutes, Tom,' I told him over the radio.

'I'm watching you. I'll keep you in sight.'

This brief conversation seemed to shake Sheila out of her private thoughts. 'Oh,' she said quickly. 'Are we landing soon?'

'Afraid so,' I told her, smiling. 'All good things come to an end, unfortunately.'

'It's just that I had a special request.' She bent down to the knapsack she'd brought along and took out a large silver container – a flask of some type.

'Don't tell me you brought your own coffee along,' I said laughing. 'We supply all that, you know.'

'No,' she said seriously. 'I've brought along my father's ashes to scatter on the trees, if that's all right.'

If there was ever a right time to be embarrassed, this was it. I should have guessed this wasn't an anniversary flight – the two of them were much too serious, and now it all made sense. Of course – she's scattering ashes!

'I'm so sorry,' I gulped. 'Yes, by all means. But we are landing soon. Maybe you should do it now before we leave all the trees behind.'

Sheila turned outwards again to look down at the forest. 'Dad absolutely loved the fall colours,' she said softly. 'He's been so ill recently and he's not been able to get out. But his dying wish was to have his ashes scattered over the trees in their brilliant fall colours. I'm so grateful to you for helping us make it happen.'

Norris placed a protective arm around his wife as she opened the urn and prepared to empty it over the trees below. A respectful silence fell over the balloon, and their private ceremony was under way.

'Goodbye, Dad,' she whispered as a tear fell to her cheek. 'I love you.'

It was a touching ceremony, done with class and reverence. But it was totally ruined in an instant through nobody's fault. The silence was shattered by an urgent message from Tom, coming loud and clear on the radio.

'Jon, there's a load of black crap falling out of the balloon! Not sure what it is but it could be something burning.'

I was stunned, and for the second time I was totally mortified. Sheila looked around, still wiping her eyes.

'Really,' she said. 'That's just too much.'

'I'm sorry again,' I stammered. 'Tom wasn't to know. He's watching the balloon very closely at this stage of the flight, and he's expected to report anything unusual. Maybe he should have been told…'

'It's all right,' she sniffed. 'It can't be helped.'

We went through our landing procedures and touched down at the first opportunity. I ended up quite far from the road and Tom and Mark had to drive a fair distance into the field. Sheila and Norris had already climbed out of the basket by the time the Ram reached us and I motioned Tom over handing him the crown line so we could begin to deflate.

'Don't mention the black crap,' I whispered. 'They were scattering ashes.'

He stared at me blankly. 'You mean the black stuff falling from…?'

'Yes, it was her father's ashes. She was scattering them over the forest to fulfil his dying wishes.'

Tom paled on hearing this news, and as the implications of his unfortunate comments sank in, he too was thoroughly embarrassed. He wanted to go over to where Sheila and Norris were standing in quiet conversation to apologize.

'I'd leave it for now,' I advised. 'Maybe you'll have an opportunity later. Don't worry about it. It's not your fault. There was no way you could have known.'

As we finished loading the trailer, Norris approached and helped me lock up the tailgate. 'That was a good flight – I survived! I never thought flying in a balloon would be so smooth. I was thinking we'd be blown about up there.'

'By the way,' I told him. 'We do have a champagne picnic ready. It's entirely up to you, of course. If you like, we can set up the table now and celebrate your first balloon flight.'

'I don't think so. Sheila's a bit weepy at the moment, and I think she'd rather go straight home.'

We dropped them off in Duffins Creek some time later. Sheila thanked us all for helping her accomplish her mission, and Norris gratefully shook all of our hands. We watched them walk over to their car, parked nearby, and a few minutes later they drove away.

'Another flight to remember,' Tom observed dryly.

'Yes, indeed,' I said. 'Whatever will they ask balloonists to do next?'

~

The moraine is several miles wide in some areas between the Niagara escarpment in the west and the Trent River in the east. Hikers and horse riders are provided with an idyllic environment for their activities, and no one could imagine that such natural beauty with its rolling hills and valleys could be the source of any difficulty or inconvenience for anyone. But nature can use such land features to whip up some strange air currents that cause problems for unsuspecting balloon pilots.

Simon Wills called me occasionally to pass on aeronautical information, or to sublet flights for two that he was unable to accommodate. During one such call, he told me about a frightening experience he'd had and warned me to be wary when flying in certain locations.

'I was flying south from Mount Albert with eight passengers one morning,' he explained. 'As I crossed the moraine east of Musselman's lake, I was staying fairly low, enjoying a smooth and level flight. Suddenly, the balloon began to fall rapidly and no amount of burning seemed to make any difference. I thought we'd hit the ground, but luckily I was able to break the fall at a mere fifty feet. It was pretty scary, I can tell you.'

'What do you suppose would cause that?' I asked.

'I can only put it down to severe downdraft. If there's any significant surface wind the air will be forced upwards as it hits the moraine hills, and on the other side, you'll get severe downdraft. You can be in serious trouble if you're too low.'

I was interested to hear about this phenomenon, but as I'd crossed the moraine a hundred times or more without incident, I wasn't particularly concerned or worried about it. In fact, I completely forgot about it until one day Mother Nature finally caught up with me.

I was flying from our Mount Albert site with Beth and Joe, a giddy young couple who were totally enthralled with their first ballooning experience. They laughed and joked between hugging and kissing, pointing out landmarks and familiar places as we drifted along.

I maintained a steady altitude of about 500 feet over a stretch of thick forest to allow them to look at the geese on a small lake to the west. 'There,' I said, pointing it out. 'Musselman's lake.'

Suddenly, the Skylark was falling. Unconcerned, I blasted heat from one of the burners. It made absolutely no difference. Again I blasted, and as we fell like a stone, I used both burners in an attempt to break the fall. The forest below came ever closer and I continued to burn furiously until we finally hit the treetops with a crash.

To my dizzy passengers, it was the most hilarious thing that had ever happened to them. But as they squealed with laughter and excitement, the enormous amount of heat that I'd pumped into the balloon took effect. We shot out of the forest like a cork from a bottle, soaring up to 2000 feet at an alarming rate. I was quite shaken as the Skylark finally stabilized and I regained control – but not my passengers.

'That was amazing,' cried Beth, entangled in Joe's arms and barely able to contain herself. 'Can we do that again? Please – oh please!'

'I don't think so. That little stunt wasn't planned.'

The balloon was gently falling now. We'd crossed the moraine and a few likely fields began to appear. As we'd been flying for more than an hour, I decided to touch down in a pasture that lay directly in my flight path. It was an L-shaped field, bordered by tall trees that provided protection from the wind, allowing me to execute an impressive soft landing on the lush grass.

'That's more like it,' I told my passengers, who would have been more than happy to continue the flight. 'That's the way to land a balloon.'

I gently feathered the burners to keep the Skylark inflated until my chase crew arrived but something caught our attention.

'What's that noise?' Joe was looking at the row of trees that hid most of the pasture from us. We heard what seemed to be the thundering of hooves on the ground, becoming ever louder and closer. Suddenly they appeared as they rounded the corner a hundred yards away – a herd of a dozen or more black shorthorn bulls, furiously enraged and charging the basket like a brigade of engaged cavalry.

'Oh my God!' Beth crouched down in the basket, clinging tightly to a propane tank with Joe close beside her. 'These bulls are going to mow us down!'

I'd never encountered such a problem before, but instinctively I blasted both burners, desperately trying to get off the ground. The bulls showed no sign whatsoever of slowing down and I feared the worst.

'Come on! Come on! Give me lift.' The response was painfully slow, but after what seemed like an eternity of burning, the Skylark began to rise. We escaped in the nick of time. As the herd reached us we were barely ten feet above them, and they snorted angrily and pawed the ground, watching us take to the skies once more.

Beth and Joe were quickly on their feet again. Now, feeling safe in the rising basket, they resumed their uproarious laughter. They looked down at the raging bulls below, delighted and thrilled at their close encounter.

'I've never had so much fun in my life,' Beth shrieked, shaking with glee and excitement. 'Do you do this on every flight?'

We had been well protected by the trees bordering the bulls' pasture, but as we rose above the treetops I found that the wind increased considerably, and we moved along at a healthy clip. There were several large fields a mile or two ahead and it was a simple matter to choose one for our final landing. As I approached, I laughed to myself as I realized we were going to have a drag landing on top of all the other adventures we'd had on this remarkable flight.

'Grab your handles,' I told the giddy pair. 'This basket is going to tip.'

We hit the ground with a jolt and the basket fell to its side and sped across the grassy field, bumping and bouncing along until we finally came to rest. The three of us lay there tangled together, laughing hysterically as we tried to extricate ourselves from one another and crawl from the basket. This had been a most unusual balloon trip, and it amused me enormously to think that Beth and Joe took it all to be quite normal, as if I'd carefully planned every detail.

It took some time for Sean and Fergus to find us. They'd seen my rocket-like take off from the forest followed by our descent into the bulls' field and they'd assumed we were still in there somewhere. When they found an angry herd of bulls but no balloon, they continued driving until Fergus spotted us in the open fields to the south.

'Looks like you're having fun today,' Sean laughed. 'We saw you shooting for the moon back there.'

Beth couldn't wait to tell them about the bulls, and as we sipped champagne in the cool morning air, she entertained us all with a re-enactment of everything that had happened during the flight. It was an exceptionally boisterous celebration, which was quite fitting, because I was delighted to have been able to provide such an exciting experience for this young, adventurous couple.

As we dropped them off at their car in Stoneville, Beth and Joe were still as high as kites after their eventful flight in a hot-air balloon.

'This was the absolute best thing I've ever done,' Beth told us exuberantly. 'I'm going to tell all my friends about it so you can expect some calls.'

'That's fine,' I said, 'but just make it clear that shorthorn bulls are not part of the deal.'

XV
NEW PLANS AND NEW PILOTS

'We'll need to go up at least 10,000 feet,' said the caller. 'My buddy and I are experienced jumpers but we've never baled out from a hot air balloon before. Do you think you can arrange it for us?'

'Well, I'm not sure. You'll probably have a lot of heavy equipment. What kind of weight are we talking about?'

'You should count on about 250lb each when you take the equipment into account. Neither one of us weighs over 200lb but our 'chutes and all the accessories are quite heavy. Count on, say, 500lb total for the two of us.'

'That's pretty close to the limits, but let me give it some thought,' I said. 'The balloon is approved for parachute jumping, but I've never used it for that purpose. I'll have to get some advice and read up on the recommended procedures.'

This was certainly something different, but it sounded like fun and I was interested in pursuing the idea. I phoned Simon immediately to see what he thought.

'It can be done,' he told me, 'but you have to do it right. First thing you'll have to check out is the air regulations concerning high altitude flying.'

'Yes, I know. Anything over 13,000 feet requires oxygen equipment, but what about the balloon's limitations.'

144

'You'll need to get into a rapid fall before they jump, and let them go one at a time. If you suddenly lose 500lb you're liable to shoot up like a cork from a bottle.' Yes, I thought, I know all about that.

After discussing the possibilities with Simon, I felt confident about taking the parachutists to high altitude for their skydiving event. I called them back with some details.

'We should be able to arrange it if we can get the right kind of day,' I told them. 'It'll cost $500 for the two of you.'

This seemed to be a major problem. 'Five hundred! Holy gee! They only charge us $35 each to jump from a plane.'

I explained the difference to them – the expense of flying a balloon, the insurance, the crew and chase vehicle needed, and so on, but to no avail. They hadn't realized that jumping from a balloon would be so expensive and the whole thing was called off.

I could have written off my negotiations with the skydivers as a complete waste of time, but my research into the possibilities for parachute jumping led to some new ideas for Skylark Balloons, and I started to think about some other possibilities. Perhaps we could have a bigger balloon as well as the Skylark, I thought, then, besides having the capabilities for carrying more passengers, we'd have more room for special projects like aerial photography or skydiving. But then we'd need two pilots as well.

Tom had often talked about getting his balloon pilot's licence, but he spent all his ballooning time with me, and I wasn't qualified to train him. I decided I could do something about that and I broached the subject with Tom.

'Are you still keen on being a pilot yourself?' I asked him one morning after we'd dropped our passengers off.

'Of course, but I don't know how I'll ever be able to do it. It's a question of time – and money.' He looked at me, expecting some follow up to my question.

'You've got a few hours of burner time, but none of it counts, because I'm not a qualified instructor. I think we should do something about that.'

'What do you mean?' he said, becoming very interested. 'What do you have in mind?'

'I'm thinking I'll ask Simon to train me as an instructor. Then I'll be able to train you as a pilot. How does that sound?'

I'd been a pilot for a few years now and I was satisfied that I had the knowledge and experience to be an instructor. It was just a question of going through the ministry programme and qualifying for an instructor rating on my pilot licence. I asked Simon if he could fit in some more training around his busy schedule, and luckily he was quite willing to take me through the course. We worked out a training schedule to take place over the following few months.

The requirements for instructor rating were obvious and straightforward. I had to conduct training sessions while Simon observed or supervised me, giving me advice on teaching techniques and making sure all areas of the curriculum were properly covered. That meant Tom could be trained as a pilot while I was being trained as an instructor – a very satisfactory arrangement for all of us.

'You know you have to write an instructor's exam?' Simon said, laughing at the irony of it. 'You're a highly qualified teacher and principal, but you have to prove to the ministry that you know how to instruct.'

'Yes, I know,' I said dryly, 'but I read somewhere that it's possible for some people with professional qualifications to get an exemption.'

'It's a possibility. Call them and see what they have to say.'

I wasn't enthused about going to write another exam at the aviation region office in Toronto, and I called one of the men with a short haircut and neat moustache to see what the situation was for someone in my position.

'We make no exceptions for anyone,' said the examiner sternly. 'Everyone seeking instructor status must pass the exam with a minimum of 80%.'

'You mean my doctorate in education doesn't count?'

'It's an impressive qualification, sir, but you'll still have to pass the ministry exam as well.'

That was that. No further discussion. I had to write the exam, and I decided to get it over with as soon as possible.

I went down to the examination centre the following day, wondering whether Amy and the uptight invigilator would still be there, but there was no sign of either one of them. I looked carefully at the envelope given to me by the middle-aged lady behind the counter.

'Are you sure this is the right exam?' I asked with a grin.

She obviously had no sense of humour. 'Of course it's the right exam,' she snapped. 'What do you take us for? We wouldn't make a mistake like that.'

I didn't care to explain the joke. I went directly to the examination room and finished writing as quickly as possible. It seemed like a waste of time, but the exam was rather easy and I exceeded the pass mark with no problem.

By the time I had an instructor rating stamped on my pilot's licence, Tom had completed ten hours of burner time towards his basic balloon pilot qualification. This was encouraging, but we both realized that he had a long way to go. As well as getting the hours in, we had to look at all the mandatory manoeuvres, emergency procedures and ground school topics. Besides that, he needed to practice his landings in all kinds of different weather conditions.

This was all quite difficult to organize between my regular passenger flights. The result was that Tom's training took a very long time to complete. For a while, it seemed that the only time we could arrange training flights was when regular passenger flights were cancelled.

~

One Sunday afternoon in late summer, Tom had been waiting for a call to confirm weather conditions for the evening flight. When I finally called him I had good news.

'The passengers have cancelled,' I told him. 'Why don't we do a training flight? The McLellan brothers can crew for us. It's a great evening – let's take advantage of it.'

No persuading was necessary. The four of us drove up to Leaskdale where we leisurely prepared the Skylark for its flight, enjoying the glorious summer evening. Things were much more relaxed when we had no paying passengers to take care of, and we took longer than usual to get everything ready.

All my crew were experienced and they knew exactly what to do. I left it all to Tom, as he was the pilot for this flight, and I looked forward to a tranquil trip in the gentle breeze.

'Take me on a balloon flight,' I said, climbing into the basket. 'You're the pilot.' I leaned into a corner, the way Simon used to do, and we were off.

'Stay low,' I told my eager student. 'I think you should practice some approaches to land and maybe touch down a few times along the way.'

The Skylark drifted south at tree top level for a few miles, but there was no opportunity to touch down. I could see a small lake ahead, directly in our flight path, and I recognized it as a depleted gravel pit on the moraine. Over the years an open pit like this fills with water from natural spring sources to create a lake, and as the vegetation grows and develops, the area becomes a veritable Garden of Eden. It's strictly private property, of course, but on a hot evening, young people sometimes sneak into the secluded area for a swim in the crystal clear water.

'How about a splash and dash on the lake?' I said to Tom, chuckling at the idea. 'It'll be a good landing practice. Just let the balloon fall gradually, skim the surface of the water, and then come up again.'

'Sound like fun. Why not?'

A grassy stretch of flat ground, perhaps a hundred yards long, lay before the edge of the lake and Tom managed a smooth descent to its surface, coming to within a foot from the ground. With the shelter of trees behind us, the Skylark moved along this stretch at a snail's pace, allowing us to take in the tranquil environment. Bird calls echoed across the water, and I was struck by the eerie beauty of the place.

'The Garden of Eden,' I said, with a laugh. 'That's what they should call it.'

Suddenly, the picture was appropriately completed. A couple of skinny-dippers had just emerged from the water and stood before us in all their glory. They were mesmerized for a moment, totally astonished at the sight of the balloon, not knowing which way to turn.

'Good evening,' I said politely, oblivious to the fact that they were stark naked. 'Beautiful evening for a swim.'

Without replying, the two of them turned and romped over to the water's edge to retrieve their towels. They wrapped themselves frantically as we continued to approach, and then broke out into hysterical giggles as we set out across the lake.

Tom grinned broadly as he looked back over his shoulder. 'Adam and Eve, I presume!'

Both Tom and I found the training flights to be enjoyable and relaxing and we began to talk more about the possibility of buying a second balloon. The idea was that Tom would fly the Skylark and I would fly the new balloon. But first we had to find out what was available. Another Cameron through Simon was one possibility, but we wanted to explore some other options as well, and we soon had an ideal opportunity to do so.

~

As registered aircraft, hot-air balloons are subject to a mandatory annual inspection in order to ensure their safety and airworthiness. But the problem faced by balloon pilots is that while there's an abundance of aircraft inspectors at every airport, very few of them are qualified to certify balloons.

During my first years as a balloonist, the annual inspection was a frustrating affair as I searched for a qualified aircraft mechanic and then tried to make an appointment for the long, detailed inspection. It wasted a huge amount of time and frequently caused the cancellation of several flights. But eventually I discovered a talented and highly skilled manufacturer who was qualified to inspect and repair hot-air balloons, and the annual inspection finally became something to look forward to.

Blaine and Sharon ran a highly organized and sophisticated operation, manufacturing hot-air balloons for sale and distributing them throughout North America. They had won several awards for their highly creative designs, and as they were the only balloon makers in Ontario, their work was in big demand. They were located in Kinneff, a small town nearly two hundred miles west of Duffins Creek, but the drive was well worth it and Tom and I would make a day of it once a year. We were fascinated with Blaine's workshop and the new ideas he was continually developing, and we greatly looked forward to the annual trip to Kinneff.

'The annual inspection's coming up soon,' I reminded Tom one day. 'I can't wait to see what Blaine's up to. Maybe we can get some ideas for a new balloon.'

It was an early morning drive, frustrating at first as we fought the Toronto rush hour traffic, but as we reached the relatively quiet countryside to the west we could appreciate the peace and tranquillity of the country lanes. We were greeted enthusiastically as usual when we reached the workshop in Kinneff. Sharon in particular bubbled with energy. She reminded me of Laura – always happy and always ready for a joke.

'Ah, the man from Leeds,' she exclaimed as she let us in. 'How's the world treating you?'

'The woman from Bradford,' I replied. 'Not bad – how are you?'

The fact that she was from Bradford and I from Leeds was always good for a few digs, and then we'd compete to see who could do the best Yorkshire accent.

Blaine and Sharon had purchased an old church and given it a new lease of life by converting it into the ideal workshop and residence. The nave provided a long open area on which to spread out balloons for inspection. Long tables containing sewing machines ran the full length of the church on either side, and the staff of busy workers sewed new balloon envelopes into place, following intricate patterns and using fabric of many colours. It was a sight to be seen.

Tom and I dragged the Skylark envelope in and deposited it on the floor. We had the whole day, and we knew Blaine would take care of the inspection when he was good and ready. 'What's new, Blaine?' I asked. 'Any new designs this year?'

'Oh, we've been experimenting with a few special shapes,' he said modestly. 'But I have a new basket design downstairs that you'll be interested in.'

Blaine was uncommonly talented and skilled. He prided himself on being able to manufacture every part of a hot air balloon, including burners and frames, baskets and envelopes. He motioned us to follow him down to the church basement. 'Come and see,' he said.

We were always fascinated with the basement. This is where the baskets were constructed, though Blaine always insisted on calling them gondolas.

'Strictly speaking,' I'd tell him good naturedly, 'gondolas go with helium balloons, and when they're under a hot-air balloon they're called baskets.'

It made no difference. As far as Blaine was concerned, his magnificent creations were gondolas.

It was a sight to thrill any balloonist. Several baskets were spread around the huge floor space, all in different stages of construction, and a skilful worker was busy weaving the wicker into place. Completed burners were neatly stacked on wooden shelves, and coiled flying wires, rolled bolts of leather and bales of wicker were ready for use on the work tables.

Blaine led us over to his latest creation. It was a large, rectangular basket, partitioned by a T shape into three sections, one of which was designed as the pilot's compartment. The other two sections were big enough to carry three passengers each.

'We're just finishing the stress tests on this gondola,' he said proudly. 'It's designed to carry six passengers in addition to the pilot.'

I was awestruck. 'Blaine, it's absolutely magnificent. The luxurious leather trim, the sturdy frame. Wow! I must have one of these.'

Blaine smiled at my enthusiasm. 'You'll need a bigger balloon than yours to carry it,' he laughed, 'but get in and check it out – see if you can imagine flying it.'

I eagerly climbed into the pilot's compartment and felt the comfortable convenience of having everything close at hand. The fuel tanks were stored away neatly, the instrument package and radios were handily located, and the burners were set away from the passengers. This would be sheer luxury.

Blaine had things to do and he left Tom and me to admire his new creation.

'This is amazing,' I said. 'Imagine what we could do if we had this. We could even put a skydiver in each side and they'd have all the room they'd need for equipment and everything.'

We spent an hour or more talking about the possibilities and checking out all the other exciting equipment under construction before finally going for lunch at the local golf course clubhouse.

By the time we returned to pick up the newly inspected Skylark, it was getting late, and we still had to face a three-hour drive home. There was paper work to complete and certificates to review, then, after a few hurried goodbyes, we left Blaine and Sharon's curious church and we were on our way, very satisfied with the day's work.

'I feel like someone who's just been to check out luxury cars in the showroom,' I said thoughtfully as we hit the highway. 'It's great to dream about the things you'd like to have, but in the end it's all a question of money.'

Tom agreed. 'Blaine's balloons are the best you can get, but they're expensive, and at the moment, I can't even think about buying one.'

I knew what he meant. Tom had already told me he'd recently separated from his family and I knew the financial situation was tight. As for me, I'd finally recovered my investment after buying the Skylark. I'd have to think carefully before committing myself to another huge financial responsibility. I didn't mention the new balloon again for some time.

XVI
DOCUMENTARIES AND DOTTY DOCTORS

I'd never felt the need to do much advertising for Skylark Balloons. After my first year, word of mouth seemed to provide all the business we could handle, and once the company was listed in the Yellow Pages, we were never short of enthusiastic passengers. But I received a telephone call one evening that led to a higher profile for Skylark Balloons than I could ever have imagined. Somebody wanted us on TV.

'We're making a documentary programme about unusual sports and activities,' said the caller who identified himself as Adrian Coe. 'We've finished a few sections like white-water rafting, bungee jumping and rock climbing, and we'd like to do one about hot-air ballooning. If you think you might be interested, we'd love to meet with you to discuss the details.' I was gobsmacked. This sounded like fun and I was immediately taken with the idea.

Tom and I met with Adrian and the producers of the programme the following week, and over too many coffees we worked out a plan of action. Adrian was the star of the show, it seemed. He was a dynamic, full-of-fun type of man who actively participated in each of the unusual sports he presented on the programme. He had impressive shots of himself hurtling down mountain streams, hanging precariously from dangerous cliffs and supposedly doing a bungee jump from an enormously high railway bridge.

'I want to do something similar with a hot-air balloon,' he told us animatedly. 'Something that will maybe bring out the danger aspect of ballooning.'

'But it's not really dangerous at all,' I protested. 'Flying in a balloon is remarkably safe and serene, and you can't really compare it to bungee jumping at all.'

'Ah, but people think it's a dangerous sport. Lots of people are afraid of heights, so the very thought of going up a few thousand feet in a wicker basket is enough to chill their blood.'

We laughed at this portrayal, but we got the idea. Adrian wanted to do some play-acting, making out that he was extremely brave to undertake such an adventure. But I was a little wary.

'I'd want the programme to encourage viewers to come ballooning with us, not put them off,' I said. 'Can't you emphasize the fun aspect of hot-air ballooning?'

Adrian could see our predicament and he changed his tack.

'Don't worry,' he said. 'I'll be emphasizing the recreational side of your sport. I've done this with all the others. The idea is to encourage participation.'

Over the following three weeks the details were worked out. We decided on an evening flight, choosing three alternative dates in case of bad weather. There'd be cameras on the ground and in the balloon, and all aspects of the flight, from inflation to landing, would be covered. Adrian would be with me the whole time, both on the ground and in the air, asking questions and making comments for the benefit of the viewers. It was an exciting project and we looked forward to it immensely.

~

'It looks like we chose the right day, anyway.' Tom spoke cheerfully from the driver's seat of the Ram as he sat by the open window. 'We'll never get better weather than this.'

He was right. It was a beautiful, calm evening in September, and we were waiting for the film crew to join us in a large field, three miles north of Duffins Creek. The hay had been cut and the farmer was delighted to give us permission, especially when he heard we were filming for TV. He was soon on hand, chatting excitedly with us as if we were international celebrities.

'I've seen you flying over,' he told us proudly. 'I thought you might've landed here before now.' He paused for a moment, studying us carefully. 'Do you think I might be on TV?'

I smiled at his excitement and genuine interest in the balloon. 'I'm sure you will if you hang around. I'm expecting the film crew to arrive any time now.'

We didn't have to wait long. A large box van followed by two expensive looking cars drove slowly into the field and joined us at the south end.

Adrian emerged from the Cadillac looking every bit the TV personality and flashing his trademark smile. He looked around for a while, exchanging bits of conversation with his crew, and finally came back to me. 'Looks like we're all set to go. Let the show begin!'

It was a remarkable two hours that followed. Everything moved along so smoothly that I felt none of the anticipated apprehension about my every move being filmed. Adrian was a master of his profession. He asked appropriate questions, made some hilarious statements, and brought out all the pleasing attractions of hot-air ballooning. He presented ballooning as a wildly exciting thing to do, exaggerating his faked apprehension and courage for the best effect.

The breeze was so gentle and calm that we travelled no more than three or four miles, and I managed to execute the softest landing I'd ever done, much to Adrian's astonishment. The whole project was a resounding success.

Adrian finished up by talking directly to the cameras. 'If you see a balloon in the sky,' he said, 'it might very well be the Skylark. Give Jon a call and make arrangements to participate in this amazing sport.'

The cameras were turned off. Adrian turned to me, and with a broad smile, he threw his hands in the air. 'I survived!'

It was very gratifying to watch a flight with Skylark Balloons on TV. The documentary was put together with exceptional skill and expertise, and I was delighted at the prominence given to fun and safety. I knew it would rouse interest about balloons, especially as the programme seemed to appear on TV several times, and I expected some calls because of it. I wasn't disappointed, but one call stands out in particular because it led to a very strange flight indeed.

'Hello, my name's Margot! I saw you on TV,' the caller said excitedly. 'I was absolutely amazed. I never realized that ordinary people could go up in a balloon.'

'Oh, yes,' I told her. 'We do a lot of passenger flights, especially at this time of the year. Did you want to book a flight?'

'Absolutely!' she said adamantly. 'I taped the programme and I keep watching it over and over. I've decided it's one thing I'm determined to do.'

'That's great, then. Is it a flight for two?'

'Oh, no. It's just for me. My husband wouldn't dream of doing such a thing. Anyway, I wouldn't let him. He'd totally ruin it for me.' She laughed loudly at her own joke.

This was an unusual approach, I thought, chuckling to myself at the lady's exuberance. Flights for one were not usually economical for me, but I knew that my niece, Jen, was arriving from England the following week, and I'd promised her a balloon flight during her stay. She was a flight attendant with British Airways and she thought flying in a balloon would make a welcome change. I could perhaps take Jen and Margot together.

'I'm sure we can arrange a flight for you, but it won't be for a couple of weeks,' I told Margot. 'How does that sound?'

That was fine. We decided on an early morning flight and I marked it on the calendar. As far as I was concerned, it was just one more flight booking and I wouldn't have given it another thought except for a phone call that came out of the blue a few days later.

'My name's Dr Jenkins,' he told me in a shaky voice that made me think he was quite elderly. 'I understand you've arranged to take my wife for a flight in a hot-air balloon.'

'Er… we have a flight booked for Margot Jenkins next Sunday morning. Is she your wife?'

'Yes, she is. I'm calling to tell you that I disapprove. I've told her to cancel but she refuses, so I thought I should call you myself.'

This stumped me momentarily. 'You mean she has a medical condition that would prevent her from flying,' I asked gingerly.

'No, it's not that. I just think it's too dangerous!'

This was most unusual and I had to think quickly how to handle it.

'I don't think you should worry about safety,' I assured him. 'I've taken hundreds of flights and we've never had any problem. Margot was very keen on flying in a balloon. Maybe you should let her decide. She can call me if she wants to cancel.'

Dr Jenkins wasn't very happy with this but he reluctantly agreed that his wife should be the one to decide. I hoped his apprehension wouldn't lead to any flight problems.

My niece, Jen, had arrived from England, and having heard so much about hot-air ballooning, she was eager and excited about her first trip. Naomi decided to assist Tom who was the designated chaser for the Sunday morning flight.

The aviation weather report was very positive and wind conditions seemed to indicate a pleasant flight to the north-east. Everything looked good. We met our passenger at the Glasgow site, but my heart sank as we drove into the field. Dr Jenkins had decided to accompany his wife to see her off.

'Good morning,' I called cheerfully. 'All set for your flight?'

Margot was wound up and raring to go. 'I can't wait,' she said excitedly, rushing over to the trailer to examine the basket. 'Is this it?'

Dr Jenkins had been leaning against his car, arms folded, but as we chatted he wandered over to the trailer to join his wife. He was not what I had imagined – much older than Margot and looking a bit like Santa Claus with his enormous fluffy white beard.

Margot introduced him. 'This is my husband, Harvey,' she said simply.

With a straight, unsmiling face, he shook my hand. 'Dr Jenkins,' he said.

Jen and Margot were fascinated with the inflation process and eagerly assisted in preparing the Skylark for its morning flight. We were all busy and involved. Even Dr Jenkins showed some interest, occasionally checking the karabiners and burners, shaking his head and tutting loudly. Finally everything was ready and we prepared for lift-off.

Tom and Naomi held us down as we developed some buoyancy, and then released us on our journey. 'Have a good flight,' Tom said cheerily. 'See you in an hour.'

Jen had her camera ready. She took a quick shot as we rose from the ground, and we were on our way. I imagined this parting picture would be one of stark contrast – Tom smiling and waving happily and Dr Jenkins looking sad and worried, as if he were seeing his wife for the last time.

'Harvey is so paranoid,' Margot told us as we settled into a steady flight at 1000 feet. 'He tends to ruin everything for me. He's well past retiring age, but he forgets I'm twenty years younger than him and I want to enjoy myself. Well, there was no way I'd let him spoil my balloon flight.'

'So he's retired then?'

'He still has a few private patients, the wealthy ones, but he's given up the general practice that he's had for more than thirty years.'

We soon forgot about Harvey and concentrated our attention on ballooning. We could see for miles as the early morning sun touched the countryside around us, and the farms and meadows came to life. The views were very familiar to me after doing so many flights in the area, but Margot and Jen were spellbound, as all my passengers tended to be. I still drew great satisfaction from the thrill that passengers experienced on flying in a hot-air balloon for the first time.

'Let's fly low for a while,' I said as we reached the mid-point of flight. 'If we're lucky we'll see some interesting wildlife in the woods.'

I allowed the balloon to fall steadily and we scanned the fields before us for any signs of life.

I could see a long field ahead. It appeared to be a hay field with the hay all cut and collected and I thought a gentle skim close to the ground would be fun. It was a big mistake. I realized too late that it was muck-spreading season, and this field had been generously covered. The stench was unbearable.

'Sorry,' I exclaimed. 'My mistake!' We all broke out into fits of laughter as I blasted the burners for a quick getaway.

As we slowly rose from the field, a white-bearded figure ran in from the road, waving his arms wildly and shouting incomprehensively.

'My God!' said Margot in disbelief. 'It's Harvey. What on earth is he up to now?'

We couldn't wait to see. I could see the Ram parked at the roadside, but we were off again into the clear blue sky, flying to who knows where in blissful peace and tranquillity.

Margot was spared her husband's neurotic antics as we continued our leisurely flight. She fulfilled her dream, feeling quite special to have a pilot and a flight attendant taking care of her, and by the time we were ready to land she was one happy and contented lady.

'Well, isn't that a sight for sore eyes?' I said delightedly, looking at the immaculate estate property half a mile ahead. 'What a perfect place to land.'

The large house exuded character and class as it stood on the edge of its five-acre spread. A large, landscaped pond lay between the house and the road at the front, and an enormous meadow, backed by tall trees, extended from the back. It was a simple landing and we floated leisurely to ground level, touching down softly at the bottom end of the meadow.

'Back to earth,' I said to Margot. 'Congratulations on your first flight.'

'It was absolutely marvellous!' she oozed. 'I'm over the moon.'

There was no sign of the Ram yet, so Jen and Margot helped me get the deflation under way by using their collective strength on the crown line. This worked well, and between the three of us we made good progress, but I wondered what was keeping Tom. I called him on the radio.

'Skylark to Ram – come in, Tom.' There was no reply. He was obviously out of the truck. Perhaps he's still getting permission to enter, I thought, but as I moved away from the basket the radio suddenly came to life.

'Ram to Skylark – I'm reading you.'

'Tom, is everything ok?'

'Everything's fine. We're being treated like celebrities here at the house. It seems that the owners are patients of Dr Jenkins and they've welcomed us with open arms.'

I couldn't believe it. That was some coincidence. I knew Harvey was suffering from some extraordinary nervous tension and I hoped his patients would somehow calm him down.

'Why don't you two go up to the house?' I told Jen and Margot. 'It sounds like they're having a party up there. I'll finish off here and Tom can come down with the Ram when he's ready.' They left me in peace and I spent the next fifteen minutes packing the envelope into its bag, engrossed in my own thoughts.

A strange sound stirred me from my reverie. I looked up, startled, and I was astonished to see that I was surrounded by cows. 'What the heck… ' I cried out loud. 'Where on earth have you lot come from?'

They were friendly enough, curiously eying the balloon and not the least bit afraid, but they blocked me in on all sides. The balloon and basket were all ready to be loaded, and between the cows I could now see the Ram driving slowly towards me. I didn't want to upset this bovine welcoming committee, but I gently clapped my hands and was relieved to find they dispersed peacefully, allowing the truck to come through.

'I thought we were in for some trouble there,' Tom laughed as he reached me.

'I don't know where they came from,' I said, still incredulous about their sudden appearance. 'They must have been somewhere behind the trees the whole time.'

We quickly loaded up the trailer, and as we did so, Tom told me about his frustrating chase with Dr Jenkins.

'I'm so glad it's over,' he said, shaking his head in exasperation. 'It was chaos and confusion from the moment you left the ground. First of all it was difficult to get him in the truck,' Tom told me. 'He stood there watching the balloon fly away until Naomi and I had finished loading the fan onto the trailer and were ready to drive away for the chase. When he finally did get in, he kept nervously looking out of the windows, trying to keep you in sight, and he fussed and fretted whenever we lost sight of the balloon.'

'I bet Naomi had something to say,' I said with a grin.

'I thought she'd be giving him a piece of her mind, but she was very patient with him.'

Tom drove the Ram slowly forward and headed towards the house.

'Anyway,' he went on, 'I saw you approach the hayfield. I wasn't sure if you were going to touch down, so I pulled over to the side of the road to watch the balloon. The moment I stopped the Ram, Dr Jenkins was out like a flash. He ran into the field signalling you to land, waving his arms and shouting, "Land here!" at the top of his voice. When he returned to the Ram, he was up to his ankles in mud and manure and he stank to high heaven. The rest of the drive was unbearable, but he didn't seem to mind the stink. He just kept on saying, "I hope he can land that thing safely." I don't know how I didn't completely lose my temper with him and throw him out.'

Tom sighed heavily as we reached the top of the grassy incline and drove to the front of the house where the socializing was in full swing.

'Strangely enough,' he added. 'Once he met his patients here he seemed to relax and he changed completely. His boots still stink, but it doesn't seem to be bothering anyone.'

We soon joined in the celebration. Harvey, Margot, Naomi and Jen were sitting in comfortable Muskoka chairs by the pond, and the family, a retired couple and their two sons, were busy making everyone welcome, serving coffee and snacks. They seemed to be genuinely pleased to have us all drop by so early in the morning.

The lady of the house greeted me with a smile and pulled up another chair. 'So, you're the balloonist?' she said. 'Come and tell us all about it.'

We spent a pleasant hour with those wonderful people. Margot talked incessantly about her flight, and to everyone's surprise, Dr Jenkins seemed proud of her for doing it.

Tom leaned over to me and whispered. 'The next thing you know, Harvey will be booking a flight for himself.'

I grinned at that suggestion. 'Now I think that would be expecting too much.'

XVII
LIMOUSINES AND GARBAGE DUMPS

As an unwanted witness to many amorous exchanges in the Skylark, I was always astonished at the number of different ways a man can propose marriage to a woman. I witnessed so many innovative proposals and helped to implement so many elaborate plans that I became something of an expert on how it should be done.

Most of the proposals were simple enough apart from the immensely romantic decision to do it in a hot-air balloon, but for some more ambitious suitors, the balloon wasn't quite enough. They had to guild the lily, so to speak, and go over the top to make their proposal an event that would never be forgotten. These elaborate marriage proposals stand out, not only because of their creativity, but because they had a habit of taxing my piloting skills to the limit.

I'd been a balloon pilot for several years when I first heard from Peregrine Fox. He was a thirty-something corporate lawyer, and he called me to see if I could help him carry out a convoluted plan by which he would propose marriage to a special young lady. It was a bit too complicated to explain on the phone, he told me, and would I meet him at his office in Stoneville?

'Money is no object,' he insisted from the start, 'but I do need this to work out exactly right. You'll have to tell me right away if it can't be done.'

'I'll do my best,' I told him. 'What's the plan?'

Peregrine had no idea about the intricacies of hot-air balloons, but he had his plans clearly worked out in his head and he explained them to me in great detail, trusting that I'd be able to work things out for him.

'We're having a cocktail party at The Oaks, my Golf and Country Club, in July,' he explained. A lot of my lawyer friends and associates will be attending with their wives or partners, and I'll be accompanied by a young lady, Charlotte, whom I've been dating for a year or so. I want to use this party as an opportunity to propose marriage to her.'

'That sounds wonderful,' I said. 'How does the balloon come into it?'

'Well,' he went on, 'as the party progresses, we'll all be outside around the grand entrance to the Club chatting and socializing. A white limousine will roll up and I'll invite Charlotte to climb in with me. We'll be whisked away to wherever you have the balloon ready and waiting for us.'

I listened carefully, wondering where this was all leading.

'So we'll take off and you'll propose to her in the balloon?'

'That's right, but that's not all. I want you to fly us low over the golf course, close to the clubhouse where all the guests will still be waiting. They'll give us a jubilant send off as we slowly rise into the sky.'

'Wait a minute,' I said. 'You realize that balloons can't be steered as such? If we take off fairly close to the golf course, I could try to read the winds, but I can't guarantee that we'll hit the Country Club, or even the golf course for that matter.'

Peregrine looked a little disappointed. 'But you can have the balloon all ready to go?' he asked hopefully.

'We can, but why not have it ready at The Oaks and take off from there?'

'Oh no,' he said adamantly. 'I want the balloon to be a complete surprise. The short trip in the limousine is essential to my plan.'

I wondered what was going to happen in the limousine, but I didn't like to ask. Peregrine was quite clear. He had his plans and he didn't want to change them.

I knew this romantic project would be quite difficult to pull off, but it was a challenge and I was interested in trying. Even if it doesn't work out exactly as planned, I thought, it will still be a romantic flight, and Charlotte should be a delighted new fiancée by the end of the evening. Peregrine understood the balloon's limitations, especially in terms of weather conditions, and we agreed that we'd try everything possible to make the plan work.

There was no choice about the date of the flight, of course, as the cocktail party at The Oaks had already been arranged and couldn't be changed. When the day arrived, I anxiously contacted aviation weather and was relieved to find that we'd apparently crossed our first hurdle successfully – calm winds and fair weather were forecast for the afternoon and evening. I called Peregrine to put him out of his misery.

'It's a go,' I told him. 'We can definitely have the balloon ready and waiting for you. We'll contact you on your mobile phone later to give you details about the exact location.'

He was over the moon. 'Fantastic,' he said. 'I'll get the flowers and ring to you this afternoon. You'll need to hide them somewhere in the basket.'

I hadn't been expecting that little detail, but I agreed to find a place for them. 'Hope they won't get crushed,' I muttered.

None of our usual launch sites were well positioned to take us to The Oaks, but Sean, Fergus and I studied our maps and discovered an open sports field about three miles from the golf course. As long as the winds didn't change I'd have a good chance of crossing the golf course. It seemed to be an ideal location with lots of open space, and as an added bonus there was a good gravel pathway along one edge of the field, so the limousine could drive right up to the inflated balloon.

We contacted Peregrine at the Golf and Country Club and he assured us that everything was going according to plan at his end. He was hoping to leave The Oaks with his intended no later than 7.20. The limousine ride would take about ten minutes.

A SKYLARK IN BLUE YONDER

By 7.30 the Skylark was inflated and ready for take-off, but there was no sign of the limousine. We waited anxiously, wondering whether this ambitious plan could possibly work until finally we heard encouraging signs of life.

'Who's this arriving?' Sean said, looking across to the field's entrance.

A sleek, red Cadillac drove towards us, and as it reached the balloon, a well-dressed young man hopped out. He held an enormous bouquet of expensive-looking flowers in his arms and he hurriedly pulled out a ring box from his jacket pocket. 'Peregrine sent these,' he said excitedly. 'He's on his way now. Give him about five minutes.'

The messenger didn't stay to chat. He drove off as quickly as he had arrived, leaving us to cope with the cumbersome bouquet. 'How am I supposed to hide these?' I asked wryly, as Fergus carefully placed them in the basket. 'They'll be ruined.'

'Finally!' Sean was holding the basket firmly on the ground as I burned intermittently, keeping the envelope fully inflated. 'The show's about to begin.'

The white limousine drove slowly across the full length of the field to where we waited and stopped directly in front of the basket. Peregrine appeared first, looking confident and happy in black dinner jacket and bowtie. He took Charlotte by the hand and assisted her as she stepped out of the impressive vehicle, looking somewhat bewildered and confused.

'Oh my God!' she exclaimed. 'I can't believe this. We're actually going up in a balloon?'

'Yes, we are,' said Peregrine proudly. 'Hop right in.'

As soon as I saw Charlotte I realized that I'd neglected to give Peregrine one piece of essential information – how to dress.

'This girl is not dressed for ballooning,' I whispered to Sean. 'Short cocktail dress and high heels – I don't think so.'

With some assistance from Sean and Fergus, the two of them were quickly installed in the basket and I left the ground without delay, quickly rising to 500 feet. I had estimated that at this altitude I'd be able to see the golf course almost immediately, and then by manipulating the rise and fall as needed, I should be able to keep the balloon on track. With some luck I'd be able to hit the golf course, and I might even come close to the excited group waiting at The Oaks.

Within a few minutes, Peregrine was already popping the question, but I couldn't give them any attention. I had to concentrate on the delicate manoeuvres needed to at least give me a fighting chance of making the golf course. At least he didn't get on his knees and get in my way, I thought. Thank God for that.

I was vaguely aware of the romantic scene unfolding behind me as I searched the scene ahead for my target.

'Please marry me...'

'Oh, of course I will. . .'

Bouquet rustling. . . 'Oh Peregrine...'

'Darling...'

I'd heard it all before a hundred times and I left them to it.

I could see the golf course clearly now. We were too far to the right so I let the Skylark fall gradually until I was on track again. As we fell, I was delighted to see that the balloon was on a flight path that would bring us directly over the golf course. I brought the balloon still closer to the ground.

We were down to 100 feet now, and to my utter amazement the Golf and Country Club appeared directly ahead. By some miracle I was over the ninth fairway in front of The Oaks with a huge crowd of well-wishers clearly in view. I was determined not to miss this extraordinary opportunity. I landed the balloon right there with barely a bounce, and the crowd of cheering spectators came rushing forward to greet us.

It was absolute pandemonium! Peregrine and Charlotte were wild with excitement, and their friends and associates encircled us with cries of congratulations, all struggling to kiss, hug and shake hands with the happy pair. Through a combination of skill and incredible luck I'd been able to accomplish the almost impossible, and I was well pleased with myself, but none of the exuberant participants in this wild melee could appreciate it. Why wouldn't a balloon land where it was wanted?

'Well, we did it,' I said to Peregrine. 'I don't know how, but it couldn't have worked out any better. The rest of this trip will be simple. We'll take off from here and land further south in half an hour or so.'

Peregrine was delighted. 'This is far better than I ever expected. I thought we'd simply fly over The Oaks and have everyone waiving up at us. But to actually land here. That's amazing.'

With all the excited congratulations and animated conversations over, it was time to take off again. We still had almost an hour before sunset, and I envisaged a calm scenic flight at fairly low altitude, allowing the newly engaged couple a chance to relax and admire some scenic countryside.

As we rose leisurely from the fairway, the crowd broke out into wild cheering again, and we drifted away to finish this amazing trip. I could see the Ram parked on a roadway below us, ready to take up the chase once more, and I was surprised to see the white limousine parked behind it.

'Look at that,' I said to Peregrine, pointing out the two vehicles. 'The limousine has stayed with the chase vehicle the whole way.'

'I asked the driver to do that,' he told me. 'We want to be picked up when we land. The limousine will take us back to The Oaks.'

That's a different idea, I thought. I wonder what it would cost to have a limousine chasing a balloon.

Peregrine and Charlotte were one happy couple for the rest of the flight. We were low enough for them to search for wildlife and examine some familiar landmarks from a different angle. At one point we crossed a settlement of country homes where people were barbecuing in their backyards. They called up to us and waved us on. Our journey was almost complete and I radioed Sean to let him know.

I was more than satisfied with my performance, and I was still amazed at my good luck in landing at The Oaks. I couldn't wait to tell Tom about that one.

I looked at the newly engaged, standing close together and chatting quietly. 'This has been quite a trip,' I said. 'I've never done a flight quite like it.'

'I've never been in a balloon before,' Peregrine said, shaking his head in wonder, 'but boy, am I ever impressed.'

I could see some rolling grassy hills ahead. 'Unfortunately, this flight is coming to an end,' I told them, 'but I see your limousine is right with us. I'm going to touch down in these meadows off to the left.'

I dropped the balloon steadily and lined up smoothly for a landing. We were in open country now and the wind was noticeably stronger. I grabbed the deflation line firmly.

'We may tip,' I said quickly as we approached the ground. 'You'll have to grab yourself a handle.'

It was a smooth enough landing, but as we made contact with the ground, the basket tipped as I had predicted, and we were dragged gently along to the top of a grassy slope where the balloon began to deflate rapidly.

A narrow ridge at the top stopped the basket dead in its tracks. Unfortunately, Peregrine and Charlotte had let go of their handles prematurely, and the happy couple, dressed for an elegant cocktail party, literally dived out of the basket, rolled over the top and down the hill beyond.

It all happened so quickly and smoothly that I wasn't concerned about any injuries, but as I crawled out of the basket I knew from the smell that this was no meadow. I stood up to see a long, steep hollow before me, and at the bottom was a dreadfully messy garbage dump, full of all manner of refuse and rubbish. Peregrine and Charlotte lay there speechless, wondering what had happened.

'Are you two ok?' I asked innocently, looking down at them. 'Sorry – that's the way balloons land sometimes.'

They seemed to lie there for an awful long time, so I started down the hill to give them a hand, but it was just too much for someone with a British sense of humour. This could have been a cartoon from Punch Magazine – an elegant couple in formal dress, lying in the middle of a filthy garbage dump – and I suddenly started to laugh uncontrollably.

'Let me help you up,' I said, grinning all over my face. 'You'll remember the day you got engaged for the rest of your lives.'

I helped them out of the dump, and Peregrine and Charlotte began to appreciate the humour. Charlotte broke out into hysterical laughter as we reached the top of the hill. 'My shoes!' she exclaimed between the giggles. 'I've lost my shoes!'

As we emerged from the dump, we saw the Ram making its way across the field with the limousine close behind.

'Now doesn't that complete the picture?' Peregrine stood with hands on hips, laughing gently at his absurd quandary. 'A limousine coming to pick us up at the garbage dump – and look at us. What a mess!'

'We can't let you go without a champagne toast, despite the smell,' I told them. 'We'll do it now, and then you can be on your way back to The Oaks. I hope they'll let you in.'

Sean and Fergus quickly organized the glasses and champagne, and we all leaned around the tipped basket, six of us now, and laughed over the details of this extraordinary flight. The inauspicious ending no longer seemed to matter. We'd achieved every last detail of Peregrine's elaborate plan, and he was well satisfied. Charlotte couldn't have been happier. Their clothes were ruined, but it was an elated couple that climbed into the limousine, and we couldn't ask for more.

As they were about to drive away, Peregrine suddenly jumped out of the limousine and headed back to the dump. He'd decided he was going to look for his fiancée's high-heeled shoes before they left.

'They can't be that hard to find,' he said.

After rooting in the rubbish for a minute, he ran up the hill, grinning from ear to ear. 'Got 'em,' he announced triumphantly, holding them high above his head. He jumped into the back of the limousine and they drove off and out of the field, leaving us to pack up the balloon.

It was no simple matter. The envelope had collapsed over the edge of the dump, and we had to retrieve it carefully.

'It's bound to smell a bit after this,' Sean advised quite unsympathetically.

'Don't worry about that,' I told him. 'The Skylark has seen worse. Next flight she'll be as fresh as a daisy.'

There was still a hint of daylight left in the sky as we drove out of that field. It had been a taxing and tiring flight, and suddenly I felt completely exhausted. Somehow, I didn't care.

XVIII
MEMORABLE LANDINGS AND TALES TO TELL

'You really shouldn't be drinking champagne in this freezing weather,' Melvin said sternly. 'It could cause you some serious problems, you know.'

He was an elderly dentist and he clutched his mug of coffee as Tom and I drank champagne on a cold February morning. It had been an uneventful flight and we'd landed safely in a snowy field in close proximity to the sturdy iron gates. The packing up was all done and all we had to do now was enjoy the champagne, but Melvin kept on insisting that we shouldn't be drinking it in cold weather.

'It's the alcohol, you see. It makes you feel warmer than you really are, and then before you know it you'll get hypothermia.'

'But it's compulsory,' Tom explained facetiously. 'We'd be banned from the world association of balloonists if we neglected such a duty.' With a wide smile he boldly held out his glass to Melvin. 'Cheers and congratulations on your first balloon flight.'

Melvin wasn't impressed. 'If you must, I suppose you must,' he mumbled.

Winter flights tended to be gentle and calm and this particular morning had been no exception. Melvin had been expecting

171

something a little more dramatic. He'd originally intended to take his wife on a balloon flight, but she'd backed out at the last minute, claiming she was rather long in the tooth to be getting involved in dangerous sports. In the end I'd taken Melvin on his own while Tom chased.

The grumpy dentist was still surprised and strangely disappointed about the soft landing. 'I've heard that balloons get dragged along the ground when they land,' he said. 'I was ready for it, but you touched down so softly I didn't feel a thing.'

'It all depends on the wind,' I explained. 'We do drag landings in windy conditions, but not on a calm day like this.'

'But you must have had some hair-raising adventures in your balloon. It's supposed to be a dangerous sport after all.'

Tom grinned. 'We've had a few,' he said.

I took a long sip of champagne. 'Balloons are not about hair-raising adventures,' I said philosophically. 'Balloons are about floating gently in peaceful tranquillity. They're about soul-soothing adventures and relaxing observation of nature from the air. Anything hair-raising is considered exceptional and unusual.'

Melvin looked perplexed. 'So every landing is like the one we did this morning?'

'No, I didn't say that. Out of hundreds of flights, some landings are bound to be extraordinary in one way or another. Almost all landings are safe, but some are more memorable than others. Strangely enough, though, one of the most memorable landings I ever did was incredibly soft and gentle.'

Melvin hugged his coffee cup against his chest. 'So what happened?'

I refilled my glass, leaned heavily on the trailer and told him the story:

~

It was one of those calm evenings at the end of summer. I'd taken off from Glasgow and drifted slowly towards the south-west with a middle-aged couple celebrating a fiftieth birthday.

We only travelled about five or six miles, and towards the end of the flight I started looking for somewhere to land. There were several open fields and farms ahead of us, and as we drifted along I could see we were slowly approaching a small farm with a long field at the back. It seemed to be the perfect landing site.

A strange thing happened as we reached the yard in front of the farmhouse – the wind suddenly disappeared completely and the balloon just hung there as if it had been tethered to the ground. I let the Skylark fall gradually until I was about ten feet from the ground, right in front of the farmhouse door. Just then, the farmer came out to see what was going on. He was astonished to see the balloon just hanging there outside his front door, but he just stood there with his hands in his pockets staring at me.

'What's up?' he asked. 'Are you wanting to land here?'

'If it's all right,' I replied. 'Do you mind if I touch down right here in your front yard?'

'Be my guest,' he told me, so I came down like an elevator, as calmly as can be.

My passengers were most impressed and thought I must have had some kind of secret brake that allowed me to stop like that. But it was the farmer's comments that amused me most. As he helped us to pack up the balloon, he spoke to me quite confidentially.

'You know,' he said in a quiet tone, 'a few months back a balloon landed in my back field. The pilot came roaring in here like a bat out of hell, dragging along the ground like nobody's business, passengers thrown all over the place. You've never seen anything like it. I talked to the pilot afterwards – Simon, he said his name was – and he told me that's just the way balloons land. Well, now I know different. After watching you land here today, I can see it's a question of how much skill you've got.'

I thanked him for the complement, undeserved as it was, and promised to tell Simon to clean up his act next time I saw him!

~

Tom laughed at the memory of this incident, and even the dreary dentist managed a weak smile.

Melvin was more relaxed now and Tom filled up his coffee cup from the flask that we always carried with us in cold weather. He pulled up his collar and sipped the hot coffee, obviously wanting to hear more.

'You must have had some hard landings, though. How do you handle that?'

'That depends,' I told him. 'You have to be prepared, of course, and it can be a bit nerve-wracking, but if you follow safety procedures correctly, it's no big deal.'

'Tell him about the mudbath landing.' Tom grinned mischievously, digging me with his elbow.

'The mudbath? I think you should tell that one yourself. You're the one who watched it happen.'

Tom smiled as he recalled the incident.

~

'I was chasing that morning,' he said. 'It was early spring, and we'd wondered about cancelling the flight as surface winds were borderline at about ten knots. But anyway, we decided it was a go. The passengers were young and healthy – an engaged couple – and they were dead keen to fly.

I remember having some difficulty keeping up with the balloon. It seemed to be travelling so fast, and as time passed, the speed only increased. I knew it was going to be one heck of a drag landing and I was determined not to miss it.

But the Skylark was travelling further and further south towards Toronto, and possible landing spots were becoming few and far between. I knew Jon was looking for somewhere to land so I got ahead of the balloon and pulled over to the side of the road alongside a long, narrow field. It was obviously his last chance before hitting the city. He'd have to land in this field or it would be too late. The only problem was that it was one big sea of mud.

I stood there and watched. It was absolutely incredible. The basket hit the ground and tipped immediately, then sped across the field like a race car, scooping up mud as it went. Suddenly it stopped dead in its tracks as the deep mud anchored it down, and Jon and his two passengers shot out like balls from a cannon.

There was no question of driving the truck into that field. I squelched my way over as fast as I could and found the three of them absolutely covered in mud from head to foot, wide eyes peering out of their black face masks, and white teeth flashing from their mouths as they laughed uncontrollably.

It took us the rest of the morning to get out of that mudbath, but the passengers were thrilled by the whole thing. They thought it was hilarious. By the time we dropped them off, the mud had hardened into a thick, starchy casing around their ruined clothes, but they were still giggling as they drove away. It took us a week to get the balloon cleaned up for the next flight.'

~

Melvin was highly entertained by Tom's story. 'That's more like the kind of landing I was expecting today,' he exclaimed enthusiastically. 'But with snow instead of mud.'

'A bit of excitement like that can be fun,' I said, 'but we do try to land gently if we can. That's what most passengers want.'

'I suppose they do,' he admitted reluctantly, 'but I wouldn't have minded a drag landing. I think it would be quite exciting.'

No one seemed to be in a hurry to leave, despite the cold, and as Melvin became more animated, we were encouraged to continue chatting about our experiences with the balloon.

'Have you ever had any accidents?' he asked, apparently hoping we had some gory details to tell.

Tom looked at me cautiously and I hesitated for a moment. 'Not as such,' I said. 'Aviation law distinguishes between an accident and an incident. Accidents involve serious injury or damage – that's never applied to us. But we did have one unpleasant incident that taught us all a valuable lesson.'

Melvin made himself comfortable on the edge of the trailer. 'What happened?' he asked with bated anticipation. 'Was it a bad landing?'

I hesitated again. I rarely told this story because it was the one and only flight I'd ever done that brought me and my passengers close to disaster. But Melvin needed to hear about it. He was wishing for hard landings, but he didn't appreciate the danger, and he had no understanding of the pilot's responsibility to keep the passengers safe. Maybe he'd understand better if he knew how bad it could be when things go wrong. Tom listened with a serious expression as I told Melvin the story.

~

It was all about the weather really, I told him. I've always been careful to get every detail from the aviation weather office before deciding on a balloon flight. This particular afternoon, towards the end of July, I spoke personally to an aviation meteorologist, and he assured me that we had a perfect evening for ballooning.

'Calm surface winds, upper winds below ten knots, temperatures cooling as the sun gets lower in the sky,' he said reassuringly. 'It doesn't get much better than this for you guys.'

That was what I wanted to hear. Tom was chasing for me, and it was such a pleasant evening that my wife, Naomi, decided to help him. My passengers, a sprightly, elderly couple, were greatly looking forward to the flight.

When we arrived at our launch site in Glasgow it was still a little breezy, so Tom, Naomi and I partly prepared the balloon, then we all stood around and socialized while waiting for the wind to drop. Half an hour later the wind at ground level seemed to disappear almost completely, so we quickly inflated the balloon and I took off in beautiful, calm conditions as Tom and Naomi waved us off.

Fifteen minutes later I was astounded to see an ugly thunderstorm approaching us from behind. The weather forecast had been completely wrong! My heart pounded furiously as I saw angry streaks of lightening zapping the ground, and I looked frantically for somewhere to land. There was nothing but thick forest below me, but I knew I had to land somewhere fast. I knew also that I had to appear calm in front of my passengers. This was a supreme effort, but I managed to appear composed.

'We'll have to land,' I murmured. 'I'm afraid some bad weather's approaching.'

Thunderstorms are the absolute worst problem for any aircraft, but especially for defenceless balloons. The main danger is that the storm will suck the balloon up to extremely high altitudes where there is no breathable air, and the temperatures are constantly below minus fifty degrees. Fortunately, the Skylark was far enough away from the storm's centre to avoid this.

But I couldn't escape the raging winds produced by the thunderstorm. As powerful downdrafts hit the ground they spread out in all directions, and the Skylark was suddenly hit by their full force. I sped along fearfully at treetop level, desperately hoping for an open field. I saw a tiny patch of green grass among the trees ahead and I knew I had to make it. With every ounce of concentration I could muster up, I somehow managed to touch down on that tiny field.

It was the mother of all hard landings. The field seemed bigger once we hit the ground, but we were dragged at highway speeds from one end to the other. Then the balloon came up again as we reached the far side. It whisked the basket through a wire fence and into the trees beyond where we finally came to an abrupt stop. There were no serious injuries, but we all had a few minor cuts and bruises. I'd somehow managed to land safely in an impossible situation. Amazingly, the balloon escaped with only a few small puncture holes inflicted by the tree branches.

~

Melvin stared at me blankly. 'I don't think I'd have enjoyed that one,' he said pensively.

'Believe me, you wouldn't,' Tom told him. 'I witnessed that landing, and it was as if a giant hand had picked up the balloon and flung it into the trees. Things could have been so much worse. It convinced us all that it's the weather that makes all the decisions when it comes to flying balloons.'

'It is indeed,' I agreed. 'But in those days, no one had mobile phones. With today's technology I can phone the aviation weather office right from the site before we take off. We'll never have a terrible incident like that again because we'll always have up-to-the-minute information on weather conditions.'

It was time to go. We were all beginning to feel cold now, but Melvin looked frozen to the bone. He'd long since finished all the coffee in the flask and he was now rubbing his hands together in an effort to get warm.

'I suppose I should appreciate the tranquil flight and soft landing,' he mumbled. 'Maybe drag landings are not all they're cracked up to be.'

Tom and I chuckled at the change in attitude. We'd obviously got through to him.

'Believe me,' I told him gently, 'hot-air ballooning is about serene tranquillity, adventure and camaraderie. It's an exciting sport and every flight is different, but if you're looking for terrifying experiences you'll have to try something else like, say, bungee jumping.'

XIX
TWO FOR THE SHOW

'It's for my husband, you see. He has dreamed of flying in a balloon for a long time, and I promised him we would go for his birthday. We just need a flight for two as your advertising says.'

The thick German accent was difficult to decipher. Her name was Griselda, she told me, and her husband's name was Helmut. She'd already called me three times, wanting to make a booking, but she couldn't decide on a date. To frustrate me further, she insisted on explaining in great detail the logic behind choosing one date rather than another.

'It's his friends, you see,' she went on. 'They like to visit on his birthday so we can't go for a balloon flight then.'

'Why don't we pick a date close to his birthday, then – maybe a weekend?' I suggested helpfully.

'What good is that?' she argued. 'It makes sense to give a present on the birthday, yah? What use is a birthday present when it's not your birthday?'

I couldn't win. 'You'll have to think about it some more, Griselda. When you decide on a date, you call me then and I'll see what we can do.'

Two weeks passed before Griselda called me again. She'd decided they wanted a balloon flight on Helmut's birthday, a Sunday in April, and his friends could work around it.

'If they don't like it, that's their problem,' she told me adamantly.

With wider publicity after the TV documentary, we found our passengers coming from further afield, and we'd started to meet them in Stoneville, which was more central than Duffins Creek. The town had an extensive commercial property accommodating a flea market and stockyards, and the spacious parking facilities made it an ideal meeting place for our balloon passengers. We arranged to meet Griselda and Helmut there for their early morning flight.

We were early as usual, and Tom, Mark and I sat idly in the Ram waiting for our passengers to arrive. It was a dull, overcast sort of day, and the aviation weather office had indicated calm conditions with a cloud ceiling of 1500 feet and no precipitation. 'I'll be flying quite low today,' I told Tom, 'no more than 1000 feet. It should be a very stable flight in these conditions.'

We chatted casually as we sat there waiting. Tom had finally finished his required flying hours and we'd managed to complete his high altitude experience and cold descent under emergency procedures. He still had to write the final balloon pilot exam, and we still had to arrange for his solo flights, but passenger flights kept getting in the way. 'The end is in sight,' I assured him. 'Before you know it, you'll be a fully qualified balloon pilot.' I was about to continue but I was interrupted by an astonished cry from the back seat.

'Oh my God! Don't tell me these are the passengers!'

Mark was looking across the almost deserted parking lot. A couple had parked their truck at the far end and they were now slowly making their way towards us. They were the most enormous people I had ever seen in my life.

'Now this is going to be a challenge,' Tom laughed. 'How are you going to handle this?'

The three of us stepped out of the Ram to greet our optimistic passengers as they reached us.

'Good morning. I'm Griselda. Finally we meet,' she said cheerfully. 'This is the birthday boy, Helmut.' She laughed heartily.

The birthday boy held out a chubby hand that enclosed mine completely in its grasp. He must be more than 350lb, I thought to myself. What am I going to do? He can't possibly fly in the Skylark. And Griselda herself – she must be over 300lb.

'Well, it's nice to meet you at last,' I stammered, not knowing what else to say. 'This is Tom and here's Mark. They're crewing for us today.'

Both my crewmen sported amused, unabashed grins, which threatened to turn into outrageous giggles. It didn't make things any easier for me.

I felt completely stumped. Should I just say, you're too heavy, and send them home? I couldn't do that, but I didn't know what else to do. I found myself going through the motions.

'Well,' I said unemotionally, 'we'd better get into the chase vehicle. We're going to a launch site up in Leaskdale.'

Tom opened the rear door to the Ram and assisted Griselda into the back seat. He and Mark quickly followed her in, stifling their giggles like a couple of teenagers, and leaving me to deal with Helmut.

'Why don't you get into the front with me?' I opened the passenger door for him and, with great difficulty, he hoisted himself into the seat, puffing and panting all the while. I tried to close the door, but he was so enormous that I was unable to do so. 'Bit of a problem,' I smiled.

Helmut rolled himself further in, overlapping onto the driver's seat and the door clicked shut. I thought the Ram seemed lopsided as I walked around and occupied the remaining space on the driver's side. I still wasn't sure how to deal with my predicament in a diplomatic way.

'The weather's a lot milder now,' I said cheerfully, making no attempt to start the engine.

'Winter's gone, yah,' Helmut agreed.

I suddenly realized that the weather could be my escape route. I could blame everything on the higher temperature and explain the difficulty it caused us. 'The higher temperature affects our load capacity, you know; we have to be very careful not to exceed the limits. The balloon can only carry so much weight.'

There was no response from this observation – just a vacant stare from Helmut. I took my load capacity calculator from my flight bag, punched in some figures, and then tackled the more delicate part of my problem.

'We usually calculate on the basis of 200lb per person,' I explained. 'What would you say you weigh, Helmut?'

He looked somewhat uncomfortable with the question, but he shrugged his enormous frame and bravely offered, 'Oh, I'm over 300lb for sure, yah.'

Griselda leaned forward and poked him sharply in the back. 'You are more than 400lb, Helmut. I'm nearly 400lb myself, and I know you are at least 50lb more than me.'

That said it all. This couple weighed more than 800lb between them, the weight of a small horse, and I began to worry that they might be too heavy for the Ram, never mind the balloon.

'Well, according to my calculations, at today's temperature, I can carry a total load of 600lb, including my own weight. I'm only 190lb so that leaves 410lb for the passengers. It looks like we're out of luck. I won't be able to take you.'

The heavy twosome was clearly disappointed. 'Nobody told me about weight,' Griselda complained indignantly. 'I called you many times and not once did you tell me about weight.'

'I didn't think to ask you,' I said apologetically. 'I'm sorry, but we have to put safety first. The way things are, I could only take one of you.'

I regretted saying that immediately. If Helmut managed to climb into the basket at all, he'd fill it completely and there'd be no room for anyone else, including the pilot. Luckily, it wasn't an option for Griselda.

'We can't have only one go in the balloon,' she said grumpily. 'It's supposed to be a special treat for the two of us.'

They seemed to be making no effort to leave, as if they expected me to find some magical solution to the problem and take them for a flight after all.

An idea occurred to me. I turned around to face Griselda as she sat there, close to tears.

'One of my colleagues, a balloon pilot in Stoneville, has two very large balloons that can carry more weight,' I told them. 'If you wish, I can arrange for you to have a balloon flight with that company. It won't be today, of course, but I'm sure I can work something out for you.'

Griselda wasn't appeased. 'But today is Helmut's birthday,' she wailed. 'We were excited about a balloon ride and now it's ruined.'

Maybe it's not the greatest idea anyway, I thought. They'd have to count as two persons each and Simon might charge them double.

It took us some time, but eventually we persuaded the unhappy pair to accept the fact that they were too heavy to fly in a balloon and exit the truck. We watched them waddle over to their own vehicle, which must have been specially reinforced to accommodate them. With great effort they climbed in and drove away.

'You handled that really well,' said Tom, laughing at the absurdity of the situation. 'How could they not realize that weight would be a big concern?'

'People don't understand,' I explained kindly. 'They don't think about these things until they're faced with a problem.'

Mark leaned on the side of the truck with an impish grin on his face. 'What you could've done,' he said, 'is attach the balloon to Helmut's belt loops and send him off on a balloon flight by himself.'

'Really! You guys. . .!'

~

We'd lost our passengers but it was a perfect morning for ballooning and we weren't about to miss the chance for a flight of our own in such calm weather conditions.

'So what do we do now?' Tom asked hopefully.

'Well, I think you should do some more pilot training. You need all the practice you can get.'

This seemed to go down well. 'I'm sure you could persuade me,' he said with a contented laugh.

An idea occurred to me. Tom was definitely ready to solo and this would be a great opportunity. With an overcast sky, no forecast for precipitation, and a cloud base of 1500 feet, the flying conditions would be ideal for a first solo. I couldn't tell Tom that, of course. Solos are best unannounced.

'Let's go up to Leaskdale as planned,' I suggested. 'Mark can chase and we can do some more landing practice while we have the chance.'

The Leaskdale site was particularly good for student pilots. With wide open space and clear views stretching into the far distance, take-offs could be gradual and leisurely. I had every confidence that Tom could do a successful solo, bringing him one step closer to his balloon pilot licence.

We went through all our usual preparations and procedures, and as the pilot, Tom conducted the final safety checks from the basket. He feathered the burners, keeping the envelope inflated, while Mark and I assisted with our collective weight on the basket. The balloon was ready for take-off. Tom looked at me anxiously. 'Come on, Jon. You'd better hop in.'

'This is your first solo,' I told him calmly. 'Don't go any higher than 1000 feet. Remember the cloud base is quite low. Fly for at least thirty minutes. Contact me on the radio when you're ready to land. We'll stay with you. Good luck!'

We released the basket and he was off. He had no time to worry about it, and he seemed confident and pleased as he left the ground. Mark and I stood back and watched the ascent. It was smooth, gentle and calm, just as I had expected.

It was the first time I had ever seen the Skylark from this perspective, and it seemed very strange to watch it leaving without me. But I didn't admire it for long. As the balloon reached about 300 feet I got the shock of my life when it suddenly disappeared into the clouds, leaving Mark and me staring open-mouthed with astonishment.

'My God!' I exclaimed. 'She's gone! Right into the clouds!'

We looked at each other, speechless and confused, not knowing what to do first.

'They quoted a cloud base of 1500 feet,' I said angrily, 'but that's no more than three hundred. We've got to contact Tom – he'll wonder what the heck's going on.'

I hurriedly jumped into the truck and grabbed the radio microphone. 'Tom, can you read me? Don't answer until it's safe to do so. You've totally disappeared from view.'

There was no answer. I knew Tom would be busy checking his instruments and I gave him time to adjust. After a couple of minutes his voice came through loud and clear.

'I'm OK. It's quite a thin layer of cloud,' he said. 'I'm in brilliant sunshine up here, but below me is a sea of white cloud as far as the eye can see.'

'Great,' I thought. 'How are we going to follow him? More to the point, how is he going to land?'

This was a situation that called for calm, reasoned thinking. Mark sat in the driver's seat of the Ram, ready to go, and I sat beside him with my maps spread open. 'At least we have contact with the Skylark,' I said. 'What we need to know is what the instruments say. If Tom can keep us informed we'll be able to stay close.'

Mark drove us out of the field onto a country road running south. I held the microphone, ready to talk.

'Tom, I'll have to ask you some questions.'

'OK, go ahead.'

'First of all, what's your altitude?'

'About 800 feet.'

'It's important that you hold it steady. Can you do that?'

There was no reply for a minute. Through my open window I heard the distant sound of the burners blasting. Of course, I thought, we'll hear the burners!

'I can keep the altitude at a steady 800 feet.'

'Good. Now, what's your heading?'

'About 230 degrees.'

'Fine, so you're heading more or less to the south-west. The wind can be no more than five knots so you won't go far. We'll have a pretty good idea of where you are, especially if we can hear the burners. I'll call you in a few minutes.'

As Mark drove I gave him directions as I carefully calculated where the balloon should be, based on the information Tom had given me. Thank God he took off from Leaskdale, I thought. At least we are surrounded by open fields and he should be able to land once he emerges from the clouds.

We drove along slowly, listening for the sound of the burners. Occasionally we heard them faintly in the distance and tried to move towards them, but this proved very difficult as the clouds played tricks with our ears. I knew that as long as we had radio contact we were not too far away.

'How long has he been flying?' Mark asked, glancing at the Ram's clock.

'Almost half an hour. But he's only travelled three or four miles at the most.'

A notation on the map grabbed my attention. I noticed that a tall radio tower was marked near Sandford, and as we were heading in that direction, I thought it might be a useful landmark. The top might be visible above the cloud base, I thought, and if Tom can see it, that will help us to identify his position.

'Tom, can you see anything ahead besides the clouds?'

After a moment's silence his voice came through again. 'I can see a tower peeping through about a mile in front of me to the right. It looks like a radio tower of some sort.'

Bingo! I knew exactly where he was now. 'Tom,' I called excitedly, 'you're approaching some pastures and meadows around Sandford. I want you to start falling now. Keep your descent steady at about 100 feet per minute until you can see the ground again. Start now.'

As we approached Sandford, Mark pulled over to the hard shoulder and I stepped out, microphone in hand, staring at the cloud-covered sky over the fields ahead. I was delighted to hear a burner blast, loud and clear. 'I think we've done it,' I called to Mark. 'We should see him any minute.'

It was a long minute, but I was enormously relieved to see the Skylark emerge from the clouds as pretty as ever, drifting slowly towards the empty meadows ahead.

'Tom, I can finally see you. Thank God for that. Are you OK?'

'I'm fine. It's been a great flight. I'm coming in for a landing.'

We continued our chase, much more relaxed now, and found easy access to a large pasture where Tom did the perfect soft landing. It had been a nerve-wracking flight from my perspective, but Tom didn't seem to mind at all.

'The view was awesome,' he told us excitedly. 'It was like being in a jet plane at 35,000 feet with all the clouds beneath me. I never really worried about it. Anyway, the landing was fine.' He threw up his arms. 'My first solo,' he cried triumphantly.

'Congratulations!' I said. 'But it's not over yet.'

'What do you mean?'

'You'll see.'

I wasn't going to let him avoid the initiation ceremony. That would be an affront to balloonists everywhere. Anyway, I remembered mine with great affection, and I knew that Tom would enjoy the celebration, messy as it is.

The three of us packed up and loaded without delay. When everything was ready, Mark retrieved the packed hamper from the Ram.

'This belongs to Helmut and Griselda by rights.' He held up two bottles of champagne and a picnic of strawberries, Dutch cheese and crackers.

'I doubt if they'll need it,' I laughed, and then looked at Tom menacingly.

'OK, balloon pilot, kneel down.'

We went through the balloonists' initiation rites, celebrating once more the incomparable experience of flying solo for the first time. Tom's solo had been most unusual – scary in fact – although he took it in his stride. He came to no harm, but I knew such a thing should never have happened and I was determined to learn from this experience.

'Next time you fly to blue yonder,' I said, holding my champagne glass high, 'I'd like you to do it without actually touching the clouds! Here's to aviation weather forecasts. May we always take them with a grain of salt!'

XX
GUNS, VEGGIES AND POT-BELLIED PIGS

'We have to keep the farmers and landowners on our side. Without them we can't operate. But it's mostly a question of helping them to understand and respecting their wishes, especially where animals and crops are concerned.'

Simon was showing me his Ordnance Survey maps and how he had marked off some prohibited zones – p-zeds, as he called them. As he was flying three balloons, he and his two pilots came into contact with landowners several times a week and over the years they had collected lots of information about the way things should be done.

'With very few exceptions,' I told him, 'I've had nothing but friendly welcome and cooperation from farmers. I'm always careful and I always try to get permission before deflating. We've had lots of farmers join us in a glass of champagne. Some have even invited us to land on their property again – if only that were possible!'

I enjoyed these informal chats with Simon when we met by chance at one of the launch sites. We'd leave our respective crew men to get the balloons set up, and we'd take the opportunity to compare notes and trade ideas. But this time he was a little more serious. He insisted on giving me the map coordinates of the p-zeds so I could mark them down.

'I've been flying this area for twelve years,' he explained, 'and I've always had cooperation too, but we've had a couple of mishaps lately involving cows. The farmers have asked us to stay at 1000 feet over their farms, and we should respect that.'

'That's fine,' I said. 'It's easy enough to do – I'll mark all the p-zeds on my maps.'

I thought no more about it, and over the following few weeks I took the usual precautions and tried to be careful as animals and crops began to appear in the fields. It was only on Tom's second solo flight that I learned first hand what Simon had been getting at. Fortunately, we had a silver-tongued chaser to see us through.

Peter Broderick still chased for us when he was available, and it was always a pleasure to have him involved. His sense of humour and lively personality kept our spirits high and he always seemed to add an extra dimension of fun and excitement to every flight. This time I wondered if we would have been able to save the day without him.

Tom took off from Mount Albert that morning, and as it was his second solo flight, all the hoopla and bustle of the first was unnecessary. Peter and I saw him off safely and wished him good luck. I still felt a little anxious at seeing the Skylark lift off without me, but I expected it to be a straightforward, uneventful flight.

'Keep out of the clouds,' I yelled mockingly as he sailed above the treetops.

It was a leisurely chase and the Skylark seemed to follow a familiar path to the south-west, drifting lazily in the calm winds. I knew Tom was a good, safe pilot. He'd done dozens of landings with me by his side, and I had no worries or concerns about his abilities. After thirty minutes, the prescribed minimum, he contacted the Ram.

Tom's confident voice came through clearly. 'I'm going to start looking for a landing spot. Are you with me?'

'We've got you in sight,' I returned. 'We'll follow you in.'

Peter drove slowly along the country roads as we tried to anticipate the Skylark's landing spot. After a few minutes we could see the balloon descending in a smooth flight path, burners blasting intermittently, as Tom came in a couple of fields north of the road.

It looked like an excellent soft landing and we could see the Skylark standing there majestically at one end of the pasture. There were no animals or crops in sight and I was pleased that he'd been able to find a field where no harm could be done. There'd be no unhappy farmer to deal with here.

'Great landing,' Peter said excitedly, shading his eyes to get a better view. 'Why did I ever give it up?'

'That was your choice,' I said unsympathetically.

It was a large farm in an isolated spot. The old farmhouse lay at the end of a long, straight driveway lined by tall trees, and we confidently drove in to find the owner. This was the normal procedure for chasers. Permission first – then follow the owner's directions for access.

'I think it'll be pretty straightforward,' I said. 'It's a big, open field, and we should have no problem driving right to the balloon.'

I called Tom on the radio. 'We're driving in, Tom. Should be with you in a minute. Just getting permission. Great landing, by the way.'

'Thanks. I'll start deflating.'

Peter drove to the top of the driveway and stopped outside the tree-shaded front porch. 'Stay there,' I said. 'I'll see if there's anyone home.'

I slammed the truck's door and started towards the porch. As I reached it I was startled by a deep, menacing voice. 'Stay right where you are.'

I stopped dead in my tracks and looked towards the corner of the small frame house where the voice had come from. My heart was suddenly pounding from the shock. A heavily bearded man in leather jacket and black Stetson stood there, looking through the sights of a rifle that was aimed directly at me.

'Is that your balloon back there?' he asked gruffly.

It was difficult to reply under such pressure. 'Yes, it is,' I managed to say in a strained voice. 'I was just coming to get permission to retrieve it.'

'I'm just about to blow holes in it. Who said you could land it here?'

Peter stepped out of the truck and walked slowly to my side. The rifle was still pointed at us and he eyed it warily, wondering what kind of man we were dealing with.

'We don't want to cause any harm or inconvenience,' he said calmly. 'We can leave immediately if you don't want us here.'

The man lowered his rifle so that it was pointed at the ground. 'I'll say I don't want you here. This is private property. Why did you land here?'

'We have a student pilot flying the balloon,' I explained as calmly as I could. 'He saw the open field and thought it would do no harm to land there. Obviously, we'd need your permission to drive out to him.'

'You'd better tell him to take off then. And you can get the hell off my property.'

The Skylark was hidden from view by the heavily wooded area around the house, but I knew it was too late for Tom to take off again. The balloon was probably half deflated by now, and to re-inflate it we'd need the fan. We'd have to drive out into the back field anyway. We'd burnt our boats. We had to persuade this man to let us in.

The surly owner walked towards us with his rifle still pointed at the ground. 'I don't like strangers,' he said. 'I live here because I don't want to be bugged by anyone.'

He suddenly seemed a little more human.

'I can understand that,' I said sympathetically. 'I can promise you we won't land here again. We can mark your property on the maps as a no-fly zone.'

This cooperation on my part did little to appease him, and we spent the next fifteen minutes listening to his rant about how he didn't want to be disturbed by unwelcome strangers dropping in.

As we talked the tension eased a little, but we still had to retrieve the balloon, and we were no closer to getting permission to enter the field. Tom was obviously wondering where we were. His voice boomed impatiently out of the open truck window. 'Skylark to Ram. Where the heck are you?'

I walked back to the truck, wondering if I was going to be ordered to stop in my tracks again, but to my relief, no such command came. I quickly grabbed the microphone. 'Bit of a problem, Tom. Give us a few minutes.'

As I walked back I noticed a small barn beyond the house and two or three long, rickety tables that had been set up on either side of the open doors. They were loaded with baskets of vegetables and Peter was eying them with great interest.

'Are you a vegetable farmer, then?' he asked kindly, appearing genuinely interested.

'Not as such.'

'But you do have a lot of fine-looking crops on the table there. What are they for?'

The man sighed deeply. 'Not that it's any of your business, but I grow some veggies to sell at the farmers' market in Stoneville. That's how I make a living – such as it is.'

'It's just that I was going to pick up fresh vegetables on the way home today,' Peter went on enthusiastically. 'Mind if I take a look?'

Without waiting for an answer, he walked briskly over to the tables and began to examine the loaded baskets, admiring them loudly with intermittent whistles.

'These are fantastic. Come and look at these, Jon. I've never seen anything like it.'

I walked over to join Peter, followed closely by a more relaxed landowner. They seemed like very ordinary vegetables to me, but Peter kept talking as if they were the last word in market gardening.

'How do you get such quality?' he asked. 'These potatoes and carrots – they're unbelievable.' He looked at our bearded friend and held out a hand. 'Peter, by the way – and this is Jon.'

'Lloyd,' he said reluctantly. He tapped Peter's hand but avoided a handshake.

Peter picked up two baskets of potatoes and two baskets of carrots. 'Can I buy some of these? Jon, don't miss out on a chance like this.' He thrust a few baskets of green beans and some small tubs of tomatoes into my arms.

Lloyd could hardly refuse. Within a few minutes we'd bought half his supply of vegetables and he was soon busily loading them into the back of the Ram. The hostilities rapidly evaporated as money changed hands, and I was happy to see Lloyd putting the rifle safely inside his front door as he went to get change. The crisis was over.

Peter looked at me with a slight smirk. 'He'll be fine now. He'll let us go through.'

A few minutes later we were driving into the back field where we found Tom leaning on the basket, arms folded and looking rather bored. He'd packed up the balloon single-handedly and had everything ready for loading.

'What kept you?' he asked, a little annoyed at being left to do the whole job himself. 'Have you two been socializing again while I do all the work?'

'Don't ask,' I said grimly. 'It's a long story. By the way, do you need any veggies?'

'Veggies?'

'That's a long story too. I'll explain once we're out of here.'

There was no sign of Lloyd when we drove out of the field. The place looked deserted, just as it had done when we arrived, so we headed out to the road with no goodbyes. I was happy to leave and I hoped I would never have occasion to come back. In more than eight years of ballooning I'd never had anyone point a gun at me before, loaded or not, and it left a bad taste in my mouth.

'Well, at least you've got veggies for the next month,' Peter joked as we finally got on our way.

'Six months, more like,' I grumbled.

Tom looked puzzled. 'So what happened back there? What's all this about the veggies?'

We told him the whole story on the drive home. He was shocked to hear about the gun incident, but he laughed heartily about our vegetable shopping and how it had saved the day. 'Never a dull moment for balloonists, eh?'

I laughed with him. 'I must say you do some very interesting solo flights,' I said. 'If you're not flying into the clouds, you're taking us into wild west country – guns and all.'

~

With his solos done, Tom had finished his training, and a few weeks later he passed his ministry exams with no problem. He was finally a fully qualified balloonist.

'The longest training programme in balloon history,' he joked when he proudly showed us his pilot's licence one morning. 'It's taken me over three years to get my licence, but here it is. All I need now is a balloon.'

'Maybe we should take another trip down to Blaine and Sharon's workshop,' I suggested hopefully.

Tom looked at me with a pained frown. 'Not likely,' he said. "I've got no money.'

I knew he was still having financial problems and struggling with family maintenance payments, so I left it at that.

'Not to worry,' I said. 'You can always fly the Skylark now that you're qualified – as long as you promise to keep well away from Lloyd's farm.'

We still joked among ourselves about the incident with Lloyd and his gun, but deep down it bothered me quite a lot. Even though it was only one bad experience out of hundreds of landings, I couldn't get it out of my mind, and for a long time I worried that something similar could happen on subsequent flights.

Fortunately, nothing did happen, and over the following weeks, as we were welcomed and assisted on almost every landing, my conviction about the friendly nature of Ontario farmers and landowners was gradually restored. Of all the friendly receptions we received, however, one incident stands out as an example of extraordinary generosity and amity.

Having Tom as an extra pilot made it much easier for me to give occasional flights to my crew. Sean, Fergus and Mark were all keen to take to the skies and I started to leave blank spots on the calendar so that the five of us could create balloon adventures of our own. These flights were inevitably fun-filled and usually ended at one of our favourite country restaurants where we'd mull over every detail of the flight and drink endless cups of coffee.

On one such occasion, just before Christmas, Tom had taken Fergus and Mark on a flight from Leaskdale to Queensville while Sean and I chased. It was a pleasant, uneventful flight on a cold December morning, and Tom had no difficulty finding a good landing spot with easy access for the truck.

Following our usual routine, Sean went to seek permission to enter, but there seemed to be no one home at the modest farmhouse. In this situation we had to assume permission, and we drove into the back field to get started on the deflation and pack-up.

The temperature was hovering around zero and we worked quickly, anticipating breakfast with hot coffee at Country Style on the way home, but as we were almost ready to leave, we were startled by a woman's voice calling from the open gate. 'Sorry I couldn't come to the door when you knocked,' she shouted. 'I was busy in the back kitchen.'

She walked briskly towards us, beaming with a smile that seemed to cover her entire face, and I walked to meet her.

'We were trying to get permission to enter,' I said apologetically. 'We thought there was no one home. Hope you don't mind.'

She laughed heartily. 'I don't mind. I've seen you flying over and I was hoping you'd land here one of these times. My name's Beryl,' she said. 'I've always wanted to look at one of these balloons close up.'

'Too bad we've finished packing everything away,' I told her. 'You could've climbed in the basket and we'd have been happy to show you how it all works.'

'Could I really? That would have been great.' Beryl seemed quite fascinated with the whole idea of flying in a balloon and she walked around the basket, asking questions and examining the intricate weaving and neatly padded top. When she had finished her inspection, she stood back with her fists on her hips.

'Now,' she said firmly, 'you all look frozen out here. Why don't you come in and have a coffee to warm up a bit?' She smiled broadly as she looked at us, turning her head to each in turn.

'That's very kind of you,' Tom said, returning her smile. 'Are you sure it's no trouble?'

'Of course it's no trouble. I wouldn't have asked if it was. Come with me.'

We accompanied Beryl to the farmhouse while she chatted merrily, wanting to know each of our names and how long we'd been flying balloons.

'What does my farm look like from the air?' she asked curiously. 'I've always wanted to get a picture of the house from up there.'

We removed our muddy boots as we entered the house and Beryl led us into her humble living quarters where a blazing log fire was already warming up the room. She invited us to find a seat on the long sofa and well-worn easy chairs.

As we shuffled around, trying to squeeze into the limited space, we stared in astonishment at the vision before us. Lying on the carpet in front of the fire was an enormous pot-bellied pig, snoring contentedly and quite undisturbed by our noisy entry.

'This is Wilbur,' Beryl laughed, giving him a friendly poke with her toes. 'He's lovely and warm so just rest your cold feet on him – he won't mind.'

She bustled away to the kitchen, calling over her shoulder, 'I'll soon get that coffee pot rolling.'

Mark found the idea of having a pet pig in one's living room to be absolutely hilarious, but he eagerly accepted the invitation to warm his feet on Wilbur's exposed belly. 'She's right,' he chuckled. 'He's as warm as toast.'

Within a few minutes, Beryl was back with huge mugs of steaming coffee. 'Here we are,' she announced. 'Hope you like it strong.' Wilbur sighed heavily, stretched himself out to his full length and resumed his snoring. 'Don't mind him,' Beryl laughed. 'He loves the company.'

Sean leaned back into his chair, touched by our host's generosity. 'Beryl, this is so kind of you,' he said sincerely. 'The farmers have always been good to us, but this really takes the biscuit.'

'Well, I'm a bit like Wilbur, you see. I love company too.' She laughed jovially at the comparison and headed back towards the kitchen. 'Now,' she said, 'I'm cooking up some bacon, so I trust you'd all like a bacon sandwich.'

We'd never been treated so graciously, but a cartoonist would have had a field day with the irony of the scene in Beryl's living room that morning – five balloonists huddled together, drinking hot coffee and eating bacon sandwiches – whilst warming their feet on a pot-bellied pig!

We were all in fine spirits and our drive home was even more boisterous than usual. 'What a life,' I said. 'Another great ballooning experience and Christmas just around the corner. What more could you want?'

'And I'll never hear another word against Ontario landowners,' Tom added emphatically. 'They're the best.' We all enthusiastically agreed with that.

This was our last flight before the holidays and we wished each other the season's best as we went our separate ways in Duffins Creek. As usual, Tom and I hung around for a few minutes and watched the others drive away. He seemed a little preoccupied as if he had something to say, and he suddenly blurted it out.

'I have to go away for a while,' he said hesitatingly. 'My company's doing a job in Milton and they want me to go down there and supervise it.'

'Oh – well that's good news, isn't it?'

'Well, yes and no. The thing is, I won't be able to do any ballooning for a while. Milton's a good sixty miles from here – it would be a long drive early in the morning.'

'So how long will you be away?'

'Six months to a year, probably. We're building a water treatment plant so it depends on how fast we can get the job done.'

This took me by surprise. 'Six months to a year! So you mean you'll be living down there? How will Skylark Balloons manage without you?'

We talked about it for a few minutes, but Tom seemed anxious to be on his way. He'd come back for an occasional evening flight, he explained, once we'd got through the long winter, and he promised to stay in touch.

'I'm not giving up ballooning,' he said with a forced smile. 'It's really the only thing that keeps me going these days.'

I watched him walk sadly to his car. There's something wrong, I thought. There's something he's not telling me.

I didn't know it then, but that would be the last time I'd ever see him.

XXI
CHAMPAGNE, FRIENDSHIP AND CAMARADERIE

'I'm not retiring, I'm superannuating,' I said emphatically. 'There's a huge difference, you know.'

It was one of those staffroom discussions, and as the time for my departure rapidly approached, the questions about why I'd want to retire so young became ever more frequent. I had decided long ago that I'd retire from my school administration job as soon as I was allowed to do so under the Ontario Teachers' Pension rules.

I loved my job enormously, but I had other things to do in my life. Why would I want the daily stress and strain of being a school principal when I had the choice of superannuation? I still planned to be involved in education, but I could spend more time on Skylark Balloons as well. I wouldn't be retiring – I'd be moving on to other things.

'But there's one thing I'd like to do before I leave,' I told my teachers. 'I'd like to organize a staff balloon flight – get us all up in the sky for a leisurely evening adventure and finish up with a champagne celebration in a country meadow.'

My suggestion was met with great enthusiasm and excitement. This was my last school. I'd been there for two years and the staff had become used to hearing about the latest balloon happenings every Monday morning. They were always eager for another story, but the thought of actually flying in a balloon themselves had never occurred to them.

'But how many passengers can you take?' they wanted to know.

'I can only take two in the Skylark,' I admitted, 'but my colleague, Simon Wills, can take twenty passengers in his three balloons. We can all take off together, and after landing we can meet in a pre-arranged place for a champagne picnic and a rowdy hoopla.'

Over the next few days I managed to work out a date that would suit both Simon and the teachers, and we picked a rain date as well to avoid any disappointment. By the time we had all the details settled, eighteen teachers had signed up for the flight. They waited patiently, checking the weather forecast each day and developing a bit of healthy nervousness and anxiety as the flight date came ever nearer.

As luck would have it, our first date was a blustery day with plenty of thunderstorm activity and strong surface winds – definitely not a day for ballooning, much to the disappointment of everyone. This meant waiting another week and coping with a bit more nervous anticipation.

The rain date arrived with much better weather, though the surface winds were stronger than I would have liked. I discussed it with Simon in the late afternoon. We had to make a decision on whether to fly or not as everyone involved needed to be informed as soon as possible.

'I think we should go,' I said resolutely. 'We may have a drag landing, but so what? Our passengers are all healthy people, younger than I am, in fact, and it will provide a bit of extra excitement for them.'

Simon agreed. 'As long as surface winds are below the ten-knot mark there's no reason why we shouldn't fly. My two pilots will have to make their own decisions at the site, of course.'

It was a go. We all met at a campsite near Sandford – eighteen passengers, four pilots and assorted crew. I'd never seen my staff so exuberant. Almost as soon as we arrived, everyone was eagerly involved in preparing the balloons for flight. I'd been unable to contact Tom, but Fergus and Mark were there, joining in the palpable excitement of the group and enjoying the attention they received from so many first-time passengers.

Once all four balloons were fully inflated we loaded our passengers and prepared for simultaneous launch. A signal from Simon saw us off. It was an amazing spectacle as four balloons left the ground together and rose grandly to our agreed altitude of 1500 feet for the flight south. For the first few minutes the ecstatic passengers were able to call from one balloon to another, until we finally drifted too far apart, making inter-balloon conversations much more difficult.

It was a pleasant hour in the air. I had flown with other balloonists several times before, but it was quite unusual for us to take off together. Some finely tuned piloting skills were needed to stay close during the flight. By using radio contact between ourselves we could at least share information, especially when we were searching for suitable landing sites.

As landing time approached I was pleased to see that all four balloons had at least stayed within sight of each other during the flight, allowing us to touch down in the same general area. I saw one of Simon's balloons touch down first. It was a breezy landing and I could imagine the exhilaration of my teachers as they were dragged along the length of the field.

As I approached to land I saw Simon's second balloon about to touch down in a field to my right. It seemed that Murphy's Law was being firmly applied. There was one tree in the field and the balloon seemed to be heading directly for it. But as I concentrated on my own landing, I quickly lost sight of Simon's balloons, though I knew they were all close by.

Much to the delight of my two passengers, the Skylark tipped in the surface breeze as we made contact with the ground, ending up by a large iron gate next to the road. Fergus and Mark were already there and they rushed in on foot to help me keep things under control. We wasted no time, and before long we were packed up and on our way to the camp grounds at Musselman's lake where we had arranged to have our champagne picnic with the others.

The level of elation and excitement was extraordinary. As we sipped champagne and nibbled on strawberries, pâté and crackers, everyone had a story to tell, and everyone talked at once. We'd all had bumpy landings; one basket scraped the trees as the balloon came in on its final approach; another tipped basket travelled the length of the meadow before coming to an abrupt stop. Everyone had experienced something new and extraordinary – something they'd never forget.

The excited babbling went on until dark, and then we continued by the headlights of the four chase vehicles. It was a fitting culmination to a wonderful staff experience.

It was only as we finally prepared to leave that it suddenly dawned on me that this celebration marked the end of my formal career in education as well. I had but one month to go as a school principal.

~

It was a relatively quiet summer for Skylark Balloons that year. A few flights were cancelled because of frequent thunderstorm activity, but apart from that, I had a lot to think about and I kept the bookings to a minimum.

As September drew near I looked forward to my new freedom. I planned to do something special on the first day of school – something to mark my first day of freedom in an appropriate way. But before I had time to give it any serious thought, Simon called me with an urgent request.

'I have four young people just out of high school wanting a balloon flight on the first Tuesday in September,' he said. 'I have no pilots available. Do you think you could take them for me?'

'That's school opening day,' I told him with a contented chuckle.

'I know, but since you're a man of leisure now, I thought you'd like to do it.'

'And the other problem, of course, is that the Skylark can only handle two passengers.'

'Yes, you'll have to fly one of my balloons. I'll pay you normal pilot's rate.'

It sounded like a great idea and I agreed immediately. Instead of fighting traffic on the highway heading for school, I'd be in blue sky watching the fall creep in.

It was an early morning flight and I met the two young couples at Simon's headquarters in Stoneville, along with Beth, a muscular young woman whom Simon had assigned to chase for me. The young passengers were thoroughly excited about flying in a hot-air balloon and they eagerly greeted me as I arrived.

'So, you're ballooning instead of going to school, are you?' I joked, shaking each hand in turn.

'College doesn't start for another two weeks,' they informed me happily. 'We've finished with high school.'

I chuckled at their elated good spirits. 'Don't worry,' I said. 'I'm skipping school too. This is my first day as a retired school principal.'

That stopped them in their tracks. They stared at me for a minute with open mouths, not quite knowing what to say, but they quickly relaxed as they realized that principals can be ordinary human beings like anyone else.

Flying with high-spirited young people provides exhilaration all on its own, and the five of us had a thoroughly enjoyable flight over the tranquil farms and fields of late summer. Although I'd been flying the area for close to ten years, it still gave me great pleasure to point out familiar landmarks like lake Scugog and the ever beautiful scenery of the moraine, but on this first day of school, the satisfaction of doing so was even further enhanced. By the end of the trip we felt we were all skipping school together.

Beth was a highly capable and experienced chaser. I was amazed to see her already in the cut hay field as I approached to land, and as the balloon came to rest after an unusually soft landing, she drove Simon's chase vehicle alongside and prepared to help with the deflation.

'Wow! I'm impressed,' I said, still standing in the basket.

She laughed good-naturedly, obviously appreciating the compliment. 'I've been doing it for years. Look at these muscles!'

The morning sun, still low on the horizon, seemed to light up the hay field, and it cast long shadows on the ground as Beth set up a small picnic table for our traditional champagne.

A young woman from the farmhouse came to join us. Beth had invited her to share a glass with us, and the seven of us stood around the table in congenial friendship and camaraderie, toasting the health and happiness of one another. I felt I was on the verge of a new chapter in my life. Ballooning had allowed me to meet so many wonderful people over the years, and it was at moments like this when we shared champagne among passengers, crew and landowners that I felt so thankful.

I raised my glass high to my youthful companions.

'There's one last toast I'd like to make,' I said. 'To schools, students and teachers everywhere.'

I looked at my watch. It was exactly nine o'clock.

~

I was puzzled about Tom. No one seemed to know where he was. It was more than eight months since we'd all sat warming our feet on the pot-bellied pig, and that was the last time I'd seen him. His mobile phone number was no longer in service; he'd moved from the only address I knew; and now the company was telling me that Tom no longer worked for them and they had no forwarding address or phone number.

Now that I was free of my day job, I was eager to develop Skylark Balloons. I wanted to rethink the idea of buying a second balloon, and I was hoping that Tom would have finished the project in Milton by now, and would be in a position to get involved again. But my hopes were dashed forever by a telephone call that came in on the last day of September.

'I'm a friend of Tom Dale,' she said. 'My name's Ellen. Tom wanted me to call you.'

I was momentarily speechless, but immediately concerned as I noticed the anxious tone in her voice.

'Yes,' I said apprehensively, 'I've been trying to contact him for a long time. Do you know where he is?'

'He's been staying with me here in Kingston. I've only known him for a few months, but I've been kind of looking after him.'

'Looking after him...?'

'He's been very sick, you know. The cancer spread so rapidly that there was no way of dealing with it. I have to tell you – he passed away last night.'

'He's passed away...?' I heard the words but I felt unable to comprehend them. 'But I didn't even know he was ill...'

'Tom didn't want you to know. You know what he was like – he didn't want to bother anyone with his problems.' She paused, unable to speak for a moment, but then went on. 'He often spoke about you and the crew and the balloon. He missed it all terribly.'

During the course of our conversation, I gradually absorbed the shock. I remembered the day I last saw Tom, just before Christmas, as he walked sadly towards his car. I knew there was something wrong. So that was it – he'd been diagnosed with cancer.

My appetite for ballooning seemed to wane over the next few days. I cancelled the flights I had booked for the following weekend and I ignored urgent requests for fall colour flights, even though the disappointment was so evident in the voices of the enthusiastic callers. Simon can take them for now, I thought. They won't have a romantic flight for two in the Skylark, but at least they'll get to see the colours that attract so many at this time of the year.

By the third week of October I was ready to call my crew together. I'd told Sean, Fergus and Mark the sad news about their ballooning colleague immediately after I'd received the call from Ellen, but we hadn't done any flying since. Now I wanted the three of them to crew for me for a special flight I planned to take. We met at sunrise as usual in Duffins Creek and set out for Ballantrae, my favourite launch site.

'Where are we meeting the passengers?' Mark asked as we drove away.

'There are no passengers this morning.'

'No passengers?'

'No,' I said. 'This is a solo flight. I want to take a flight by myself. I haven't done it for years and I feel that it's something I want to do. And I want you three to chase together and have fun with it. After the flight we can all go to our favourite country restaurant and breakfast will be on me.'

They were more than happy to oblige. I let them prepare and inflate the Skylark for me and I climbed into the basket only when Sean had it ready to go. A few intermittent blasts of the burners and I was on my way.

'This could be a long flight,' I told them as I drifted away. 'I've got four full tanks, and with only my weight it could be a couple of hours.'

I felt an urgent need to go high. I maintained a steady rate of climb, checking my variometer periodically, and after fifteen or twenty minutes my altimeter read 5000 feet. It wasn't enough. I kept burning, rising ever higher into the clear, blue sky. I felt as free as a bird – like a skylark in blue yonder. At 8500 feet I could make out the southern shore of Lake Ontario and beyond into New York state. Lake Scugog was far below me, its picturesque island now visible in its entirety, and to the north, Lake Simcoe, the city of Barrie and Georgian Bay lay at my feet.

The scenes were so familiar to me. How many times had I pointed out these landmarks to excited, romantic passengers, as they experienced the thrill of hot-air ballooning for the first time? A long stretch of the beautiful moraine was clearly visible now. I remembered the splash and dash experience in the so-called Garden of Eden. 'Adam and Eve, I presume,' Tom had said with his quiet humour as we left the embarrassed couple standing there in all their glory. I laughed at the memory of it.

I could make out the bare hills of Lakeridge ski resort as I crossed, and I remembered my first cold descent when Simon coolly put me through my paces. What a brilliant instructor he'd been. And what a great colleague he continued to be. Was it really ten years since that first flight with Brian Turner across the Yorkshire Dales? The time had passed so quickly. And so much had happened.

Over an hour and a half I mentally recapped my ballooning career, and I wondered what the future had in store for me and my Skylark. By the time I was ready to land I'd travelled over thirty miles and I was approaching some heavily forested countryside. I thought it was time to contact my faithful crew.

'Skylark to Ram. Do you read me?'

Fergus's voice came through loud and clear. 'We're with you. Are you staying up there all day?'

I laughed. It felt good to make contact with these good friends of mine.

'I'm gradually losing altitude. I should touch down in another fifteen minutes.'

There were several large farms between the wooded areas, and I established a smooth flight path that took me directly into a long, narrow field bordered by some tall evergreens. There was sufficient wind to tip the basket. This was quite helpful as it caused the envelope to deflate without much assistance and I was able to start packing it away. By the time the crew arrived on the scene the job was half finished and the four of us soon had everything ready to go.

'That was some flight,' Mark said as he locked up the tailgate. 'How high did you get?'

'Higher than I've ever been before,' I told him. 'It gave me an entirely new perspective. I looked at the world from a different point of view.'

Breakfast lasted longer than usual. We reminisced about the amazing experiences we'd had over so many years. It was hard to imagine that Tom was gone – he'd seemed such an essential part of Skylark Balloons. Things would never really be the same again. I knew that Sean, Fergus and Mark were wondering about my plans and how ballooning would fit in. As we ordered yet another cup of coffee, Sean finally asked.

'So what will you do, now that you're retired?'

'Superannuated,' I corrected him.

'Yes, of course. But what are you planning to do?'

'Well, I'm an educator at heart,' I said thoughtfully. 'I've already arranged to conduct some seminars for school principals in a few locations across Canada. I'll be going to Ottawa, Calgary and Vancouver between now and Christmas, and I'm planning many more trips for next year.'

They looked at me quizzically. I knew what was on their minds.

'But what about Skylark Balloons?' Fergus asked. 'Where are we going with that?'

Leaning back in my chair, I looked back at them wistfully and smiled.

'Ah! Skylark Balloons,' I said. 'Now that's something I have to think about.'